Power Buying

Power Buying

How
to Get
What You Expect
Without Negotiations

Godfrey Harris with Gregrey J Harris

First Edition

The Americas Group
9200 Sunset Blvd., Suite 404
Los Angeles, California 90069
USA

ISBN: 0-935047-15-8
Library of Congress Catalog Card Number: 92-38205

Library of Congress Cataloging-in-Publication Data

Harris, Godfrey, 1937-
    Power buying : how to get what you expect without negotiations
Godfrey Harris with Gregrey J. Harris.
        p.   cm.
    Includes index.
    ISBN 0-935047-15-8
    1. Consumer behavior--United States. 2. Consumer education-
-United States.   I. Harris, Gregrey J., 1962-   . II. Title.
HF5415.33.U6H37 1993
381.3'3--dc20   92-38205
                                                        CIP

Printed in the United States of America
by
Delta Lithograph Co.

TABLE OF CONTENTS

ALSO BY GODFREY HARRIS AND GREGREY J HARRIS

Talk Is Cheap

ALSO BY GODFREY HARRIS

Mapping Russia and Its Neighbors (with Sergei A. Diakonov)
The Fascination of Ivory
Invasion (with David S. Behar)
The Ultimate Black Book
The Panamanian Perspective
Promoting International Tourism (with Kenneth M. Katz)
Commercial Translations (with Charles Sonabend)
From Trash to Treasure (with Barbara DeKovner-Mayer)
Panama's Position
The Quest for Foreign Affairs Officers (with Francis Fielder)
The History of Sandy Hook, New Jersey
Outline of Social Sciences
Outline of Western Civilization

LOSING INTEREST

Husband: *Honey, did you see this?*

Wife: *The letter from the bank confirming the transfer of your father's money into our account? I read it.*

Husband: *Fine. But did you notice the confirmation slip? It shows the money reached the bank a full week before they drafted this letter telling us that the transfer had been completed. And from the postmark, it seems to have taken another three days to get the letter in the mail and two more for the letter to get to us. Now, because of Labor Day, we won't be able to move the money to our brokerage account until next Tuesday!*

Wife: *So?*

Husband: *The bank managed to find a way to earn interest for itself on **our** money during those two weeks.*

Wife: *That's not fair.*

Husband: *You're damned right it isn't fair. If we're out 10¢ on our balance when one of our checks comes in for payment, they may not bounce it, but they sure as hell like to charge a $15 fee for providing the 'overdraft' privilege.*

Wife: *I hate it when the public is taken advantage of like that. You ought to write them a nasty letter. It's not the money we lost that's so important, it's the principle. If people like us don't complain, they'll keep on getting the benefit of being sloppy or unfair or both.*

Husband: *I don't know about being nasty, but a letter of protest is a good idea. What do you think it should say?*

Wife: *Just tell them we want the interest they took for themselves. It must be around $25.*

Husband: *More like $35. But I'll figure it to the penny—14 days at a rate of 4 percent on $25,000. But what if they ignore the letter?*

Wife: *Then I'll get very mad—and you know what that can mean.*

Husband: *I do. But will they?*

Wife: *They'll be sorry they found out.*

BACKGROUND THOUGHTS

This book shows ordinary consumers how they can become Power Buyers—the individuals who always obtain full value from the fixed-price products and services they acquire. Power Buyers seem to know exactly what they want and how to devise strategies and marshal the resources necessary to ensure that they get what they expect without negotiations.

Many would automatically assume that Power Buyers are those with large budgets and deep pockets. The fact is, however, that they are not so much rich as they are resourceful; not as concerned with quantity as they are with quality; not as big as they are bright; and not as competent as they are confident.

Ordinary consumers, on the other hand, may feel sorry for incompetent or uncaring small businesses and may be intimidated by the size, breadth, and control of big institutions. Not Power Buyers. While they don't necessarily enjoy having to increase a small business's expenses or relish having to confront a giant organization with a problem, they have learned *how* to express a need, ask a question, make a suggestion, track a matter, or direct a complaint in a way that is likely to generate an acceptable response to them for the least amount of effort.

Power Buyers have also discovered what accountants have long missed on their balance sheets: The most important asset a company has is its *customers*. And Power Buyers know that *they*—not some clerk or supervisor, not any manager or officer, and not a particular board member or key shareholder—control how this asset affects the success or failure of a business.

Ordinary consumers generally lack the energy, knowledge, or patience to deal consistently with most businesses or to find the right point of entry, the right strategy, or the right way to work success-fully through the multiple companies or formidable layers of large bureaucracies. Because of the size and specialization of powerful organizations, a whole range of experts have arisen to deal with them:

- In New York City, for example, private expediters shepherd building plans through complex and labori-ous governmental processes for homeowners and small contractors alike.

- In Los Angeles, businesses have been spawned to help people obtain licenses, registrations, and other docu-mentation from the state's large and cumbersome Department of Motor Vehicles.

- In both of these cities and beyond, attorneys specialize in the rules and regulations governing U.S. immigra-tion and naturalization matters, air quality standards, zoning procedures, and other narrow areas of com-merce and daily life.

- In American communities everywhere, certified financial planners spend a portion of their time sorting out credit card problems or reconciling checkbook stubs and bank statements instead of plotting investment strategies and retirement goals.

Many consumers, of course, cannot afford to engage an expert every time a problem arises, and most have never understood the power that resides on their side of the commercial equation. In days gone by they didn't have to. Most businesses solved consumer problems by having their employees accept the axiom that "the customer is always right." Local governments reminded civil servants that voting and taxpaying citizens were their bosses and were to be treated accordingly. No longer. Today, computer processing, fax machines, voice mail, electronic message equipment, and other technological wizardry send a different signal— machines don't get things wrong, people do; organizations aren't prone to make mistakes, patrons are; public contact isn't always bad, but it is certainly costly.

As a result of the tireless work of so many electronic chips functioning seemingly effortlessly and endlessly, an attitude of superiority has invaded the thinking of many employees. Customers, for their part, often feel that they are being placated, patronized, or put off whenever they have a question, suggestion, or problem. Automated voice response systems—with their endless menus and submenus of barely comprehensible choices for touch tone telephone users—are just one more indicator that human contact is to be avoided, not welcomed. All of this is done, mind you, in the name of less cost and increased efficiency. Despite public relations specialists, a few dedicated ombudsmen, numerous hot lines, and other devices designed to make institutions less remote to their clientele, millions of ordinary consumers still feel frustrated by systems they cannot control and organizations they do not understand.

This book is intended to help ease that feeling. It has been written to show ordinary consumers how they can become *Power Buyers,* particularly in fixed-price transactions where the cost of a product or service has been established by the seller and is not negotiable. While our approach is focused on buying, we have not differentiated between the individual shopping for a family or purchasing for a business. In fact, business people have all the same problems as a homemaker in getting what they want from the fixed-price products and services they buy. Just as importantly, business owners reading this book will learn how to evaluate if the customer should be right. In our view, it is far better to recognize a Power Buyer's concern and deal effectively with it at the outset, than to have to contend with some later combination of negative comments, hostile phone calls, snide letters, bad publicity, legal action, consumer boycotts, or worse. In fact, when all businesses come to look on their customers as an appreciating asset rather than a potential liability, commerce will become fun again for all who benefit from it.

We have grouped the ideas in this book into two major blocks of information:

The Principles and Rules of Power Buying
and
The Tools and Techniques for Getting What You Expect.

Each of the principles that a Power Buyer employs is followed by a number of rules that amplify and explain the principle itself. In the second section of the book, the four major tools used by Power Buyers are amplified by various techniques employed to make the tools as effective as possible.

You can tell from the size of this book that we have purposefully not written an encyclopedia on power buying. We have also given very little attention to the subject of negotiation, although some of the rules and techniques we discuss are applicable to good negotiating practices. Our focus, instead, has been on how to obtain maximum value from a product or service once a price has been established. We wanted to find out why some buyers always get what they expect from suppliers in fixed-price transactions and others do not.

We hope that this book goes a little way toward leveling the playing field for all consumers. Let us know any of your particularly memorable experiences in fixed-price buy/sell arrangements. It will help us help others in the future.

"Do we have enough in there for
the Power Buyers?"

Principles And Rules

Each of us is always buying something—no matter what we do to earn a living or how we spend our leisure time. Some of us may be primarily purchasing on behalf of a business or organization; others are principally buying for themselves and their families. In fact, our society is structured so that nearly all of us consume something produced by someone else every day.

Power Buyers, however, continually operate on a different level than everyone else who acquires products and services. Whether seeking necessities or luxuries, durable goods or perishable items, they exude an air of confidence that suggests they expect to be treated at least as well as the seller's most important customer. Their confidence is based on the strength of three important commodities they bring to the purchasing arena— their money, their desire, and their contacts. While all of us control these same commodities, few know how to ensure that they will always yield value.

To a Power Buyer, maximum value arises when his or her *expectations* are met or exceeded. By setting goals and articulating their needs, a Power Buyer's expectations become clear.

But sometimes questions will arise, suggestions will occur, or problems will develop with the products or services acquired. Enlightened companies prefer to handle these issues simply and rapidly on the front lines of commerce—where store clerks, technical specialists, and office employees deal with customers.

Sometimes, however, satisfaction proves difficult to achieve on the front lines. Unenlightened companies abound, clerks can't handle certain types of questions, technicians can't provide a rapid response, and line supervisors can't deal with various suggestions. In addition, of course, some matters seem to escalate naturally into challenges or change into battles. By adhering to the *principles* described in this section and using the *tools* described in the next, you should increase the value you receive when doing business with the company or institution in the future.

A standard in principles
to match!

The Principles and Their Rul

THE POWER BUYER

PRINCIPLE:
EXPECT THE BEST

0   123   456   789   0

Power Buyers start from the premise that the fixed-price products and services *they* seek to acquire offer the best value for the money spent. They further believe that the money and time expended on purchases are as important to them as they are to the businesses with which they deal.

Unfortunately, ordinary consumers don't always expect to receive the best the marketplace can provide. They don't demand

- Honesty,
- Respect,
- Efficiency,
- Promptness, and
- Courtesy

in all their dealings all the time. They don't believe that they are doing business a favor by giving it the opportunity to serve them.

Power Buyers do. They like their puchases to yield a quality product or service and they like to feel good about the transaction. Gary Jennings, the novelist, described how a commoner could win the advantages of royalty in *Raptor*, a fascinating story of 5th century Europe. The key was *acting* the part:

> *If you go into* any *encounter...trumpeting yourself as a personage*—believing *yourself truly to be one*—*[then] you will be warmly greeted, expansively welcomed, treated with reverance and deference and subservience.*

Not all businesses, of course, can deal with each consumer with the same degree of reverance, deference, and subservience. No matter the appearance or attitude, some consumers *are* more important than others and some transactions *demand* a higher level of service. Moreover, some needs have a higher moral or commercial value than others. Power Buyers understand this. If you want to operate like them, ask businesses to tell you, up front, the circumstances that may lead to *your* interests going unmet or a deadline being missed.

If you are tired of operating in the dark and having to tolerate surprises in your dealings with businesses and organizations, determine what your options are at all times and don't be embarrassed about expressing your feelings.

Thank goodness they carry fake furs now!

EXPECT THE BEST
Rule: What Are My Options?

The essence of a free market system is choice—the ability to select a company, product, or service from among several different sources. So important is this principle to the success of capitalist systems that governments usually intervene whenever effective choice seems absent. Of late, the American, British, and Mexican governments have recognized that their own monopolistic control over particular services—postal delivery systems, telecommunication services, some basic industries—can drive up costs while reducing benefits to the public. These governments have either moved toward privatizing their monopolies or allowing competitive forces into the marketplace through a reduction of regulations.

Power Buyers know that one of *their* most effective weapons is their right to choose. As a result, you should be continually testing the quality of the services and the pricing of competitors—not necessarily to *move* your business, but to better express the *demand* side of the supply/demand equation. Try a different dry cleaner, stop at a different supermarket, or ask a friend about the businesses they use. For more complex purchasing needs, interview competitors about their prices and terms or circulate formal requests for quotations from new firms entering the marketplace. If you find any significant difference in what your regular supplier charges, point it out and ask for the savings.

On another level of understanding your options, always test the honesty of a sales person's recommendations. Ask whether the person's income will be affected by your decision. If you are not comfortable being so direct—something, incidently, that distinguishes Power Buyers from ordinary consumers—tell the seller you may take 24 to 48 hours to make up your mind. If the seller then tries to sow fear that you could lose the deal or deprecates your right to hesitate in making a final decision, you have a good indication that the seller is worrying more about his or her commission than your best interests.

POINT: **Be aware of what your primary supplier's competition can offer you—and make sure that your supplier knows that you know. It is one of your most effective weapons to get what you expect from the purchases you make without negotiations.**

EXPECT THE BEST
Rule: Don't Hide Your Light Under a Bushel

It will not come as a startling revelation that mistakes are made from time to time by businesses. No institution can be expected to do everything right every time. Because we live in incredibly complex worlds—filled with dozens of changing obligations and choices—requests can sometimes go unfulfilled, orders may be mishandled, messages can be inadvertently ignored, and documents can be put in the wrong place.

All of this leads Power Buyers to treat the first error made by a business as an aberration. While they note it, they don't necessarily make an issue of it. It is the second or third time the *same* error occurs that they may react differently. If, for example, they are not treated courteously or honestly, they have learned to raise the issue with a person in authority, explicitly detailing the problem and the results. Most Power Buyers also let the person in authority know that if the same thing happens in the future, the offending company may be looking for a new customer.

All companies know the cost of acquiring a new customer, but few appreciate the cost of *losing* a customer. Negative word of mouth can travel faster than the proverbial speeding bullet. Given the possibility of losing a customer and the spread of negative word of mouth comments, the offending company should react quickly and positively to whatever problem you have identified.

Giving a business a second or third chance is not an act of charity; changing consumption patterns can be costly—finding new suppliers, meeting new people, providing a new set of explicit instructions are all bothersome. So a second or third chance to get it right often makes economic as well as psychological sense.

But if you are consistently treated improperly—particularly under the same conditions and by the same people—then make your move. Let the people who count—in the losing *and* gaining businesses—know why you are shifting your trade. It may make the first company look at its procedures and, more importantly, it will make the second company more sensitive to your needs in the future.

POINT: **Let everyone know the reason you are unhappy and that you will be prepared to act on your feelings if the problem persists.**

THE POWER BUYER

PRINCIPLE:
HONEY CATCHES MORE THAN VINEGAR

0 123 456 789 0

Why are physical confrontations considered more macho, more serious, and more definitive than quiet conversations? Is it because physical confrontations, carried to their ultimate expression, involve the life and death risks of war? Perhaps. But the interesting fact is that despite the common perception of a winner and a loser in a physical confrontation, most do not lead to a clear-cut resolution for one side or the other any more than a peaceful discussion. In fact, in war there are often as many losers, on each side, as there are winners.

So, too, hard-nosed confrontations between consumers and commerce. Despite the fact that these confrontations are entirely unequal—the latter has the power to do or defer; the former has only the power to ask and hope—one side or the other seldom seems satisfied with the end result. Think back to the personal injury law suits you have read about or to the product boycotts that have caused you to skip a purchase. Once ended, spokespeople for both sides often talk about the costs incurred by everybody, rather than the significance of the victory won. The victories always seem to come at great cost—in personnel involved, in time wasted, in lives damaged, and in other unintended consequences.

Power Buyers have long realized that major physical confrontations usually leave no winners. They seek to *avoid* situations that result in confrontations as assiduously as they seek to make their points. They have merely adopted the old adage that honey catches more flies than vinegar. In other words, they believe that being *understanding* and *reasonable* can often be more effective than being mean and miserable.

The next time you need to spread honey, offer to talk positively to your personal network about a business or product. Look hard for ways to create win-win, rather than win-lose, situations. To do this, focus on how the *business* can benefit from the solution you propose to your problem. Remember that when customers treat a business well, the business wants to deal with that customer in special ways.

HONEY CATCHES MORE THAN VINEGAR
Rule: Talk is Cheap

When businesses accede to a buyer's request or exceed a buyer's expectations, they are generally perceived as fair, generous, and just. This kind of impression often leads people to talk positively about their experience. While there may be some out-of-pocket costs involved in meeting the buyer's request, the return on this kind of investment can be handsome in terms of the word of mouth advertising generated—the most effective form of promotion available.

Take the contrary case. A buyer demands some action from a business, the business takes umbrage at the demand, and a battle between the two sides ensues. The buyer may eventually win, but it will be at a protracted cost few would be willing to pay if they knew the total of those costs *beforehand*. The consumer may also eventually lose, which is decidedly worse—for one's pride as well as pocketbook. Either way, though, confrontations have a habit of becoming expensive for both sides.

The next time you need to get a supplier's attention, try the following line:

I can't wait to tell my friends how really nice you've been in helping me.

Few suppliers can resist the potential implied in those few words. If they do, however, you can remind them of the problems caused by negative word of mouth comments: "You really don't want to find out how damaging it could be if I tell everyone I know how uncooperative this business is."

POINT: **Businesses may find it more rewarding and easier to accede to a request because that sort of treatment is likely to spark favorable word of mouth commentary.**

HONEY CATCHES MORE THAN VINEGAR
Rule: Be Daring

In June 1987, the United States decided to side with Panama's political opposition to urge the resignation of Gen. Manuel A. Noriega, then the country's military leader. Noriega refused to move. To resolve the crisis, a group in Panama wanted the United States to find General Noriega a *new* hemispheric position of responsibility. They felt he could respond to the recognition and accept the new job. But, they said, if the United States continued to threaten him with the loss of military aid, economic sanctions, political isolation, and/or military intervention, Noriega's pride would cement him in his office.

No one in the U. S. government gave the idea of promoting Noriega more than a moment's consideration—and it was then only to ridicule the thought that the President of the United States would suggest a solution based on weakness. George Bush, so the reasoning went, would never reward the bad behavior of the likes of a Manuel Noriega. Was it good behavior, then, that the President eventually ordered an invasion of 26,000 troops in 1989 to force Noriega out? It may have "felt" better to the American people, but it came at a high human and material cost. Panama suffered two years of economic sanctions; some 23 Americans and perhaps as many as 4,000 Panamanians died in the confrontation. Honey might have worked so much more quickly and so much more effectively, even if it would have required a little more effort to sell the idea.

The next time you feel like suing, boycotting, or bad mouthing an uncooperative supplier, try offering to *help* that supplier instead— by sending him or her more business, encouraging new customers, or preparing a testimonial. It may sound like an expensive, degrading, or time-consuming approach, but it may prove to be cheaper and more effective for you in the long run. Asians understand the concept better than Westerners. It is the desire to provide *face*—a concern for making sure that both sides find happiness out of each transaction.

POINT: **In commerce as in politics, look for ways to make the other side feel as much a winner from your request as you will feel if they accede to it.**

23

THE POWER BUYER

PRINCIPLE:
ASK FOR WHAT YOU WANT

0   123   456   789   0

Before Power Buyers ask for any item, begin any inquiry, make any suggestion, track any matter, or launch any complaint, they know exactly what they want to achieve for the time and effort they are likely to expend trying to get it.

A simple example of this principle occurred to us recently. We sent a check to a mail order firm for three nesting dolls shown in one of their catalogues. The item itself cost $5.98 and the company tacked on another $3.95 for postage and handling. When the order arrived, the dolls didn't fit one into another as they were meant to. We had to send them back. But previous experience with other mail order firms had shown us that claims of guaranteed "refunds" apply only to the actual *cost* of the goods themselves, not to the postage and handling charges involved.

While we had no objection to paying for the original shipment— after all, we had saved time, fuel, and stress by not having to go to a store to acquire the goods—we thought it unfair to have to pay the $1.52 *return* postage, especially since the company hadn't met our quality expectations. So we asked for a refund check in the amount of $7.50 [the original $5.98 plus $1.52 postage]. We asked for exactly what we wanted and told them why—and we got it. Later we learned that it is the policy of a number of firms to refund shipping charges—but *only* if the customer asks. Very few firms, we have discovered, volunteer to make the additional payment.

In another example of asking for what you want, a client of ours protested a $35 annual charge levied by her bank as a credit card fee. She had just received the same card from another company for free. Faced with the potential loss of a good customer, the bank rescinded the charge on the spot. Had the client not pointed out the obvious advantage of going with the new company—as we assume thousands of customers fail to do—the bank would have continued to collect the fee by default.

Too often, though, ordinary consumers are not quite certain what it is they can achieve or might want—particularly before they seek some redress from a supplier. Do they want a refund, a replacement, an apology, a reward, a little sympathy, or even revenge? The problem is that if *they* don't know what they want out of their contact with a business, they have almost no chance of feeling any satisfaction from that contact. Certainly the employees of a business can't give consumers what they want when the consumers themselves doesn't know what that might be.

Therapists are forever explaining to those trying to improve a relationship to *tell* the other person what is wanted and not to assume that the other person is a mind-reader. Children know this rule well—they never stop asking for things *they* want. Adults, however, seem to have difficulty with this simple rule. Yet, it is amazing how fast matters can proceed toward a satisfactory conclusion if the buyer has first taken the time to think about a goal and then articulated it to the supplier.

ASK FOR WHAT YOU WANT
Rule: Goals Are Not Moving Targets

Too often, we have seen people seem to *change* goals in the middle of presenting their request or trying to solve a problem. Listen to this dialogue we overheard between a customer and a counter clerk:

> *"This recorder didn't work after I used it two times."*
> *"I'm sorry to hear that. Let me get someone to look at it."*
> *"I don't think I want it fixed. My uncle always says: 'Once a lemon, always a lemon.' "*
> *"Would you like a new recorder then?"*
> *"Yes!"*
> *"Fine, we will be happy to replace it."*
> *"That's nice. But come to think of it, shouldn't I also have some blank tapes because of the trouble I was caused?"*
> *"I don't know."*
> *"I think I should."*
> *"Well, we don't carry a supply of blank tapes at this facility."*
> *"And now that I'm here, I ought to have the cost of parking at the meter out there refunded as well."*
> *"I'm sorry. This isn't the Army. We don't have chaplains dispensing sympathy either."*

By expanding the goal from a simple replacement to a reward for the inconvenience, this consumer lost the cooperation of the business and lost any hope of feeling satisfied by the end result. When businesses feel a consumer can't be satisfied under any circumstances, they are inclined to do nothing.

POINT: **The more unsure you are of exactly what you want when you start an inquiry or lodge a complaint, the more unlikely it is that you are going to feel satisfaction. Know what you want—a refund in the example above or a specific amount of compensation in other cases—and stick with it until you get it.**

ASK FOR WHAT YOU WANT
Rule: "Because I do..." Just Won't Do

Some people have a difficult time explaining *why* they want something they have requested. Perhaps they have hidden agendas—deeper, more complex reasons for their requests than the surface explanations offered. Most often, though, people simply haven't taken the time to work out in their own minds *why* the goal they seek is fair and reasonable.

When a child is asked why he thinks he needs a new bicycle, parents often hope for answers they can quote to their friends or share with both sets of grandparents, such as:

- *"So I can go to the grocery store for you."*
- *"So I won't need a ride to school."*
- *"So I can get a paper route to earn money."*

These kinds of responses are rare or perhaps only heard on reruns of such venerable TV shows as "Ozzie and Harriet" or "Leave It to Beaver." Kids don't think in those terms anyway. They sometimes have trouble justifying goals. When asked why they want something, they often resort to answers such as: "Because I do, that's why!"

Buyers need more. They need to have a clear goal from the moment they make contact with a business. Would you think of asking the boss for a raise without a long list of reasons and justifications in your mind? Our publisher told us how she used the principle with customers. She was getting down to the end of her stock of the first printing of a book and did not know exactly when the second printing would be available. If a buyer gave her a plausible reason for needing a copy immediately—for a class, to discuss at a meeting, to show a client—she sent one out the next day; but if buyers didn't ask about delivery or had no specific need in mind, their orders were designated to wait for the new supply.

POINT: **Think through the reason your goal is important to you and to the supplier and then tell the supplier what you want. If you do, you are much more likely to obtain your goal!**

ASK FOR WHAT YOU WANT
Rule: Know the Other Side

Deciding on a goal sounds more difficult than it is. More often than not, it is as simple as seeking a *replacement* for a defective product. While often annoying and sometimes time consuming to return something that you had every expectation would work properly in the first place, it is usually no problem for suppliers. So long as you have the paperwork from the original sale and a clear explanation of the problem, nearly all suppliers accept defective products on their front lines for replacement without question.

Sometimes, of course, a goal becomes more involved—the defective product not only didn't work, it caused collateral damage as well. For example, the first time a table lamp is plugged in, an electrical flash scorches the outlet plate and singes the surrounding wallpaper. Now the goal of a simple replacement has to be broadened to include compensation for the additional damage. Rather than simply checking to make sure the product was in fact defective, the enlarged goal now requires a business to do technical/legal analysis: Was the damage a matter of human failure or product failure? Could a faulty product have caused the damage claimed? Is the claim for compensation itself reasonable?

Power Buyers know that complex goals can't always be satisfied on the front lines of commerce. Their first step is to find out *who* in the supplier's organization is in a decision-making position to deal with the problem they have experienced. Once they know a name and the functional responsibility of that individual, they begin assembling the evidence to justify the case they want to make. The more credible their case, the more likely a business will accede to a request. Abraham Zaleznik, in his book *The Managerial Mystique,* takes matters a step further by pointing out that dealing with a business also requires an appreciation of the psychological mind set of its employees: "The managerial orientation...[emphasizes] form over substance...structure over people and...power relationships over work." In short, make the people you have to deal with look good and feel important, while following their rules.

POINT: **Power Buyers look at their problem from the standpoint of the *business* they are dealing with. Once they understand how the business is organized and how its people deal with a problem, they can target their approach and their activities more efficiently.**

THE POWER BUYER

PRINCIPLE:
FIND OUT

0   123   456   789   0

While some hold that man's best friend is his dog, Power Buyers know that their best friend is *information*. The more they have of this seemingly innocuous commodity, the easier it is to accomplish anything they wish.

Like intelligence agents around the world, they understand that the collection of information may seem random and of limited value, but they know it can prove important to the eventual outcome of any quest. Some people use legal pads or forms to record information as it develops; others use 3"x5" cards to shuffle and stack the information collected for later comparison and easier reference.

The purpose of the information gathered is to provide the basis for devising a strategy or implementing a tactic that will work to the Power Buyers' advantage. Analyzed information may reveal a vulnerability, a precedent, a position that is not apparent from any individual piece of information standing on its own. Put simply, opportunities that never arise can never be exploited.

Information sources may be employees, other customers, competitors, press, observations, comparison shoppers, and more. If someone once observed that a woman can never be too thin or too rich, so the Power Buyer knows that he or she can never have too much information about the matter to be resolved.

FIND OUT
Rule: Keep Digging

No matter how you try, you will probably never get all the information that may be plumbed from a single source on your first try. Detectives know this. They visit crime scenes repeatedly in case they may have missed something. They ask suspects to tell and retell their stories, often several times, and relentlessly explore the discrepancies they detect in order to satisfy themselves that they have a complete picture of an event.

Even when you *think* you have all the information you need, there may still be more to come. Yes, you understood the fellow's name on the telephone, but did you get the spelling as well? Take the name Smith. Pretty simple, right? Wrong. Telephone directories suggest that the listings for "Smithe," "Smyth," and "Smythe" should also be checked for the party sought.

Another example of the need to keep exploring for information arises from a task we were doing for some Russian scientists. Despite hours of conversation concerning the *design and operation* of a pollution control experiment they were about to conduct, we failed to ask for specific details about the *anticipated* results. Because of this, we never realized that the experiment was aimed at eliminating only *one* pollutant, not the multiple varieties usually found in a waste stream. Had we understood this, our initial efforts to acquire some measuring equipment could have been targeted on just those companies making the appropriate machines.

POINT: **After you have tried every question you can think of, and after you have read back the key points you have recorded, ask the person if there is anything else pertinent that he or she can provide or that you forgot to ask.**

FIND OUT
Rule: Read It Back to Me

Information, no matter how crucial it may seem or how interesting it may appear, is useless and even potentially dangerous when it is *wrong*. Clearly, wrong information must be avoided whenever possible. Knowing that there are many different kinds of wrong information masquerading as accurate data helps:

- People don't really know something, but sound as if they do.
- People lie about something—to give themselves more time or more status. It is the reason so many will say that the check is in the mail when it really isn't.
- People create purposefully false information—called *disinformation* by intelligence services—to get the opposing side or competitors to move in the wrong direction.
- People make mistakes—all the time!

Take the problem we had when a client sent us the following fax message concerning a public opinion survey we had spent months planning for them:

"We are not ready to proceed."

As soon as we received this word, we stopped work until just before the last possible moment when the material would become obsolete. At that stage we reminded the client of the time-sensitive nature of many of the questions in the survey. To our amazement, the client responded:

"Terrible mistake. A typo.
We meant to say: 'We are now ready to proceed.'"

To guard against wrong information, always repeat what you heard and do as many Power Buyers do, never *assume* anything. Confirm what you believe; check to make sure you are right. Both help to prevent *unnecessary* errors.

POINT: It never hurts to ask questions to be sure of your facts, and it never hurts to review everything to make sure it is right. But it hurts a lot to have to do something a second time because it was wrong in the first place.

FIND OUT
Rule: Leave Them Answering

An old theatrical adage urges performers to always leave them laughing. Billy Wilder's Academy Award winning film, *Some Like It Hot,* provides one of the best examples of the phenomenon. When the character played by Joe E. Brown learns that the "girl" he wants to marry is really a man dressed as a woman to keep hidden from the film's bad guys, he notes dryly: "Well, no one's perfect." It sent countless audiences into the theatre lobbies around the world wreathed in a smile. Many smile, even now, remembering the scatter-brained millionaire taken by an image of a woman and refusing to worry about the implications of "her" really being a "him."

Power Buyers have adapted a similar adage in their quest for information: Always Leave Them *Answering.* By repeating the command, it reminds them to generate help in a telephone call, a letter, or in a personal interview, They know that the last point raised should always be an inquiry about who else might be useful to talk with about the matter at hand or where else they ought to turn. When asked directly for help, nearly everyone is flattered and few people refuse to give it.

POINT: **Always try to be both effective and efficient. Nothing should be wasted. Even a simple phone call needs to show value for the time and cost spent on it. Asking that crucial last question about what else can be done often makes the effort worthwhile.**

FIND OUT
Rule: "If you were in my position..."

Sometimes information is not easy to elicit—a person may know too much, may not know enough, or may not know where to begin. In other cases, people need a little coaxing to help get their minds and mouths moving in the direction you wish them to go.

We have some favorite ways to *stimulate* people into helping us. We phrase our questions in this way:

- *"If you were in my position, how would you solve this problem?"*

- *"If you were in my position, who would you talk to next?"*

- *"If you were in my position, where would you go next?"*

- *"If you were in my position, what would you ask?"*

That last line is one that almost never fails. For instance, it worked when an Army officer was called upon to present the government's case against a sergeant accused of stealing paint from the Quartermaster Depot at an army post. The sergeant hired a civilian lawyer to defend him at the Special Courts-Martial. At the outset of the presentation of the government's case, the prosecuting officer asked a witness: "Didn't you see Sergeant Ruffo at the Depot on the night of August 5?" "Objection," boomed the lawyer, "counsel is leading the witness." The officer tried again: "Wasn't Sergeant Ruffo at the Depot last Saturday night?" "Objection," shouted the lawyer, "same problem." The officer scowled and the members of the board hearing the case shifted uncomfortably in their seats. "Right," said the officer turning to the lawyer— the only attorney in the room—"you ask the question the way it should be asked." The president of the court nodded in agreement, the witness was asked to tell the court what he had seen on the night in question, and, instantly the evidence sought by the prosecuting officer went into the record.

POINT: **When you pose questions to people that make them feel important or enlist their empathy, they tend to be more forthcoming in their answers.**

FIND OUT
Rule: Be Quiet

While new information can always emanate from a well-placed question or an alert observation, it often comes flooding out of nothing but silence. Power Buyers know that silence—during a conversation on the phone or in a personal confrontation—can be one of their most effective weapons:

- Most people become very uncomfortable when conversation goes dead. If you remain silent in one of these pauses, the other side may blurt out information that it might not otherwise provide. Try the technique with a friend or relative and watch how often the other person fills the empty space with talk, some of which may prove useful to your concern.

- At decision times, the last one to speak is often thought to have an advantage. As a result, we find that those who want to have the last word often improve on the deal or add new information. We let them.

- Silence is also particularly effective in group situations. While others can banter and chatter away—for effect, for dominance, or for the attention it provides—the quiet ones seem to be formulating the positions that are eventually adopted.

It happened to a colleague of ours quite by accident. He was chairing a discussion for his client to try to devise a strategy for getting more U.S. budgetary support for alternate energy projects. He had assembled 15 people from Congress, the Administration, and industry to have lunch in Washington. One of the participants asked a question about the specific interest of our colleague's client in any new funds just as our colleague took a bite from a sandwich. Before he could finish chewing and swallow, someone else jumped into the silence with an assumption that was wrong, but it sparked a whole new conversation on future conventional electricity capacity—a topic that wasn't even on the agenda. Our colleague says that this proved to be the most important aspect of the luncheon.

POINT: The old adage is true: "You can't hear anything but your own voice if you don't stop talking." Equally important, when others talk you tend to learn more and give away less.

POWER BUYER

PRINCIPLE:
GET IT RIGHT

0   123   456   789   0

Those who know what they are doing—whose every move is a confident reminder of having trod the path before—usually get what they want. Those who *seem* to know what they are doing can get the same result. Both conditions describe an important attribute of the Power Buyer.

Our attorney practices this strategy whenever he has to see a client in the hospital outside of regular visiting hours. He enters every door and strides down every corridor as if he were on the medical staff. He never asks for directions, never stops to study signs, never gives any kind of hint that he doesn't belong there as much as any other person. Because he moves in a purposeful manner, no one questions his purpose. He says that looking like he fits in a hospital environment has never failed him in more than 25 years of visiting patients as part of his legal practice.

Just as the body language of our attorney gives off the kind of signals that make his work easier, so those who are unsure of their needs, of the accuracy of their facts, or of the correctness of their position usually fall short of getting what they want.

Power Buyers, by definition, always command respect from suppliers. They achieve this enviable position by getting everything *right* the first time a supplier is given an order or later when the same supplier is approached with a question, suggestion, or complaint. To achieve the same level of respect, make sure you have the numbers, dates, history, descriptions, and other pertinent details of a product's performance or the background leading up to the acquisition at hand from the start to discuss with the supplier.

One powerful buyer we know does more than just save receipts and make notes on invoices. She saves the original packaging material, cartons, and shipping labels. When she has to return something to a retail store, she puts the item in that store's identifiable paper, plastic, or specialized bag. It isn't that she can't bear to throw things away, but that she has an appreciation of the impact of a little showmanship in all of her dealings with others.

Nothing seems to convince the opposition to see your side of the equation so much as showing that you have your side of the equation together.

GET IT RIGHT
Rule: Everyone Has a File

Under J. Edgar Hoover, the Federal Bureau of Investigation was said to maintain files on millions of Americans; but it was Hoover's files on Washington politicians that gave him his extraordinary power. For fear he might leak something on their sexual habits to a newspaper or political opponent, Congress usually gave Hoover everything he wanted.

Files are power. They become the repository of every scrap of information pertinent to a quest. They contain the copies of letters, receipts, phone notes, articles, telephone and fax numbers, and everything else that will help you prove your point, make your case, or get help.

Like the proverbial pack rat, Power Buyers tend to start files as easily as they start the engines of their cars. Once a file is opened, it is filled with everything that seems the slightest bit connected with the subject at hand. Think of a file as fertile soil—not very imposing and not very useful until you want to grow something in it. But once that decision is taken, the quality of the soil becomes crucial to what you want to achieve.

POINT: **Save everything you accumulate in a separate file until all issues are resolved and you are sure the product or service operates as promised or is consumed as intended.**

GET IT RIGHT
Rule: Truth is Hardly Ever Absolute

When all the facts or pertinent data are not known or readily available—a receipt is missing, a date is uncertain, a comment can't be recalled, a name has been forgotten, a title was never revealed—learn how to *fudge* your presentation without fibbing.

It is a skill that all successful trial lawyers and journalists have mastered. To avoid being trapped by a factual error, attorneys often describe the moment something happened as "on or about...." They let friendly witnesses know that having trouble remembering a detail is an acceptable response to questions from opposition counsel. All of us have watched courtroom scenes in the movies or on television where witnesses respond with the phrase: "To the best of my recollection...." Expressed that way, factual matters that are later shown to be inaccurate are not necessarily perjurous, and those that are inconsistent are not necessarily embarrassing.

Journalists also learn that some words are useful in blurring the edges of factual situations to compensate for any unexplored details, inadequate notes, forgotten questions, or reportorial mistakes. Such words as "appear," "tend," and "perhaps" have long kept editors happy and journalists safe. They are also words that keep diplomats at their foreign posts.

Power Buyers, it turns out, can be just as clever as the most artful lawyer, honored journalist, or experienced diplomat. Without the proof to sustain their points—a witness statement, a document, a receipt, or a faulty part— they too can "seem" to recite the facts or events "to the best of their recollections." You can practice this art by rehearsing statements out loud— statements that are basically truthful if not as *complete* as you would like.

POINT: **If you don't know, don't lie, but don't stop either. Work around factual black holes by conveying information that may be incomplete but still remains *factually* correct.**

GET IT RIGHT
Rule: A Little Embellishment Never Hurts

Power Buyers in our family have never been beyond embellishing a fact or two whenever it proved useful and seemed essentially harmless to the other person.

- When Alfred Harris, the family patriarch, opened an antique business in Los Angeles during World War II, he proclaimed that the Harris English Silver Company was "Established in 1898." Well, the truth was it hadn't been; that was just the year of his birth. But by adding longevity to his business image, he hoped to attract the confidence of his prospective customers.

- When his widow finds a restaurant booked to "capacity" on an evening she wants a reservation, she generally announces, in her best authentic British accent, that it is "Lady Victoria Harris" calling. She is every bit that, even though she has never been so designated by any King or Queen. But the touch of aristocracy usually adds support to her plea that the manager has always been able to find some "accommodation for herself and her party even when the restaurant is 'crowded.' " He usually does.

- To be sure of getting attention, a member of the family has been overheard to announce that he is *Professor* Harris—when asking for help, say, of a busy librarian; or *Dr.* Harris, when he wants a parking attendant to leave his car close to the main entrance.

- One of the authors likes to have important documents notarized and sealed even when the procedure is not required—generally to add weight and authority to the contents. The same effect is gained from sending telegrams, registered letters, or using a courier service. It is more expensive, but it does have an impact.

[Because some people are uncomfortable embellishing facts, this rule may not be appropriate for everyone.]

POINT: **When you notice something that impresses others, try to find a way to use that material—even if you have to stretch the truth to incorporate it into your power buying strategies.**

BACK TO BUSINESS

PRINCIPLE:
THINK BIG

0   123   456   789   0

We learned a lot about power buying from Alfred Harris. The particular technique he used to purchase antiques on his frequent trips to London is a case in point.

He would enter a shop, look at everything available without comment, and then ask the proprietor for a single quotation on a whole array of goods. Once the price had been worked out, Harris would begin adding and subtracting pieces from the package of goods. With each addition and subtraction he would ask the proprietor how that changed the total. The bargaining over the final configuration of goods to be sold and the total amount to be paid was never prolonged. Harris's target in this elaborate game was usually one or two pieces in the package he kept putting together, taking apart, and reassembling. He, of course, never identified these pieces, but he realized that most antique dealers could not resist making a substantial sale involving an amount considerably larger than the average buyer would likely spend in any given transaction. As long as the total was great enough, Harris knew that either the target item itself or the other pieces in the package might be acquired at a bargain price.

It is a lesson we have never forgotten in studying powerful consumers. They try to buy big every time they buy something.

It is not hard to understand why. The greater the volume, the lower the unit price.

Take an order for slippers we placed for a Russian buyer. Our supplier asked one price for 1000 pairs, a much lower price for 10,000. The cost of cutting the material, verifying the settings on the machines, and overseeing the actual manufacturing process is the same—whether one pair or 100,000 pairs are manufactured. If those *fixed* costs run $10,000, it is equal to $1 a pair on a 10,000 pair run. But it amounts to only 40¢ when 25,000 pairs are ordered. Clearly, the more an item's *fixed* costs can be spread across a broader spectrum, the lower the final price becomes.

You may have no intention of keeping everything you acquire—or you may join with other firms or friends to create formal or informal *cooperatives* to increase your buying capacity—but thinking big allows you to perfect your information about the seller's pricing policies as well as his or her flexibility to deal with different situations.

"Do it right and each of you
can become a star!"

THINK BIG
Rule: "Let me have £250 worth to begin..."

A cousin of ours, Donald Wand, used to tell about the invitation-only nights at the big London gambling clubs. The casinos would invite their best customers to bring friends along to enjoy a sumptuous complimentary meal and afterwards, perhaps, try their luck at roulette, "21," or the other gambling games. While our cousin adored anything free and loved eating out with friends, he disliked gaming. He said he was gambling big time every day in his scrap plastic business and didn't need to simulate the risks and rewards during the evening. Rather than miss an event with his friends, though—and knowing what was expected of him—Wand hit upon a way to participate and stay in harmony with his feelings.

On these invitational evenings, he would stride to the cashier's cage and count out a number of £10 and £20 notes. In return he received a mound of chips which he stuffed into his pockets. He kept about 10 or so in his hand and, as he passed around the room to "check" on the activity at each table, he would riffle the pile in the palm of his left hand as if studying the bounce of the ball or the flow of the cards. As he moved in and around, he might stop, pile all of his chips on the table, then drop one or two on an even money roulette bet or play a hand or two of black jack. Soon, though, he would gather up his chips and move on, apparently dissatisfied with some aspect of the play. If anyone asked how his luck was running, he would always respond that he was holding his own.

He was, too. When the evening was nearing an end, he would return to the cashier's cage and slowly count out his chips. When the cashier announced a count of £250—give or take five or ten pounds on either side of his original stake—our cousin would smile enigmatically.

POINT: **Thinking big does not mean having to *risk* big. Staying close to a big spender—or appearing to be a big spender—can bring all of the preferred treatment a Power Buyer attracts.**

THINK BIG
Rule: Have a Fall-Back Position

Anything you buy becomes easier to obtain if you have two or more alternative markets for it. One of the authors was brousing the antique stalls in Jaffa, Israel, when he came across a beautiful, but outrageously expensive, piece of religious art. He looked at it, thought momentarily about buying it, put it carefully down when he knew he really couldn't afford it, and moved on. But nothing else he saw that day could replace the memory of that one item. The more he thought about it, the more determined he became to find a way to acquire it.

He finally figured out how. He went back to the stall and began a methodical search for other items that he might be able to sell when he returned home. By carefully calculating the cost he anticipated paying for these lesser items and the price he could hope to charge for them, he figured he would earn enough to pay for the object he wanted. It worked! Not only was he able to sell all the items he acquired, but because of the number of purchases he made that day, the final price of the religious item was considerably lower than the price originally quoted.

POINT: **The more you can buy, the better your bargaining position becomes. Since everyone is a buyer on occasion, Power Buyers learn how to become** *sellers* **when necessary as well.**

THINK BIG
Rule: "I'll take two..."

One of our wives learned that whenever she went shopping, she got much more attention and assistance from sales personnel if she picked out multiple variations of the same item. Big sales mean big commissions in many stores. Naturally, everyone wants to be as helpful as possible in these situations; often, buying big yields greater discounts or extra amenities as well. Often no adjustment in a previously accorded discount for volume is made when items are eventually returned—the shopkeeper hoping to retain the good will and patronage of such a still perceived "heavy weight" consumer for a future occasion.

We realize that not everyone will be comfortable employing this rule and those that do will also learn that it cannot be used very often before it loses its impact. But the rule does illustrate the point that buying in large volumes can mean better service as well as lower unit prices.

Just as some situations can be manipulated by smart Power Buyers, so all of them assume that no price is ever set in hardened concrete. Given the right circumstances, they are never embarrassed to offer someone in authority less for an item than the published and/or ticketed price. Empty aisles and large inventories are as much an incentive for some suppliers to deal as scuffs, scratches, tears, dents and other damage to goods on display. Try it the next time you want something you really can't really afford!

POINT: **Approach everything as a big buyer; if in some cases you can't be, you may still command the price accorded to them.**

BACK TO BUSINESS

PRINCIPLE:
MONEY TALKS

0   123   456   789   0

It is among the oldest adages in the capitalist lexicon:

Money Talks!

The meaning is clear: In societies where all things are valued in terms of their monetary worth,the offer of money in exchange for some product or service generates attention and action. But when money is only promised rather than proffered, it tends to mumble.When it is credit sought instead of cash paid, money loses its command.

Power Buyers know this. They don't deal unless they have the money arranged to *close* a transaction; they don't start serious discussions until they have a good idea what the seller needs from the transaction.

We have found that there is an important corollary to the principle that money always talks. It is this:

A Little More Money Talks Even Louder!

Power Buyers know, for example, that if the seller is given the money sought on a more advantageous schedule or is offered more money than he or she originally asked for, they receive everything sought and the little extras besides that make doing business more a pleasure than a chore.

When money isn't appropriate, an unexpected gift to staff members or management personnel accomplishes the same objective—getting the most value from the fixed-price goods and services acquired. When you have been nice to someone, it is hard for them not to be nice in return.

"I'll give you $50 cash if you sell me your suit right now."

MONEY TALKS
Rule: The Advance Payment

The lesson of the advance payment may have originated with travelers. Take the case of the transatlantic passengers on the great ocean liners. Soon after boarding and being ushered to a stateroom, these passengers would tip their cabin stewards *before* any service had been rendered or any request had been made. The smile of appreciation from the steward indicated that he understood there would be more where that came from if the level of service during the voyage was at least up to expectations. As a result, the steward's attentiveness was generally unrelenting and the service faultless. Moreover, the type of arrangement wordlessly struck between smart passengers and clever cabin stewards was every bit as professional as the protracted negotiations between labor leaders and industrial managers around a conference room table.

Try it the next time you have a lot of luggage or are in a rush at the airport. Hand a skycap $5 before he does a thing for you—whether helping you through the formalities of checking in or getting you to a boarding gate on time. He'll bust his chops to deliver you where you need to be on the expectation of earning a further reward if successful. When you are next in a hotel, give the housekeeper a $2 or $3 tip at the *outset* of your stay. You will lack for nothing during your visit, and you will have acquired the cheapest form of insurance should you leave something behind on departure. We bet it will turn up in the hotel's lost and found rather than simply disappear.

Here's another idea. Give a gift—chocolates, dried fruit, souvenirs from a trip, a gadget personalized with your name on it—from time to time (not just at the Christmas season) to the tellers at the bank, the clerks at the post office, the attendants at the garage, or the employees at any other place where you deal regularly. You'll be surprised at what this does to bring you Power Buyer treatment and how on occasion employees will bend the rules to accommodate some need you may have.

POINT: **The advance payment—whether in the guise of a tip, a gift, or an unexpected deposit—is a signal that you are not an ordinary consumer, and, it is a powerful incentive to the recipient to do even more for you than might have been originally contemplated.**

MONEY TALKS
Rule: The Additional Payment

One of our neighbors asked a painter to quote on a total top-to-bottom job—from pool house to main house. After walking around the property twice, the painter wrote down a figure and showed it to the neighbor. The neighbor seemed surprised, and the painter hastily withdrew his note pad to try to refigure his costs. But the neighbor interrupted to say that he didn't think the estimate was too *high,* but too *low.* Was the painter sure that he could do a first-rate job at the price quoted?

The painter was too stunned to do anything but assure the neighbor that it would be the best job the neighbor had ever seen. And it was. And there was more. About halfway through the task, the neighbor showed the painter a door to his greenhouse that really needed to be re-hung. Although still on its hinges, it didn't look like it would be in place at the end of winter. The neighbor asked the painter whether he might be able to fix the door. He assured the painter that he would, of course, be compensated for this extra, non-contracted task. The painter said not to worry, he would take care of that and patch the cracks in the cement floor and re-mortar the brick wall as well. When the entire job was done, both sides were happy. The painter received *more* money than he had asked for—in short, an unexpected bonus—and the homeowner had received extra services for a fraction of the cost of hiring a carpenter and a bricklayer to fix what needed fixing. Try this approach whenever you need something repaired or a little extra service from any professional you deal with.

There is another, price-related point here. Seek the best *value* for your money rather than the lowest price available. Sometimes by spending a little bit more, you greatly increase the worth of your purchase. Two old adages apply here:

- Good jobs are seldom cheap; cheap jobs are seldom good.
- The bitterness of poor quality and poor service remain long after the sweetness of low price is forgotten.

POINT: **Generosity with suppliers or paying top dollar for commodities is not a sign of weakness or evidence of being a soft touch. It is a sign of good business to get higher value for your money.**

MONEY TALKS
Rule: Leave It on the Table

Most regulars at bars and saloons know the trick: Pay for the first round with a large bill and leave the change on the table. Remember that the word "tip" arises from the first letters of the words: To Insure Promptness. It can do that and more.

For example, money left on a table or waved in the air has an amazing power to ensure both good service and total attention. Try it the next time you are somewhere that's crowded—a restaurant, a club, a bar, or a store. Make the money visible when you ask for something additional—a fresh round of drinks, some extra ice, another plate of appetizers, a little attention, and so on. You will be impressed with how helpful the server or clerk becomes, no matter the other pressures on his or her time and attention. It is simply a human reaction to strive for what appears to be the *possible* rather than lavish attention on the unknown.

When tipping isn't appropriate, look for ways to *compliment* the people who assist you. A compliment given and accepted is often a comfortable way to indicate that further outstanding service will lead the patron to bring the employee's efforts formally to the attention of a supervisor or an establishment's services to the notice of contacts. Few can resist the a chance to shine and be rewarded in this way.

POINT: **Power Buyers know that it never hurts to let people know that they expect outstanding service and to demonstrate that they are willing to reward such service when received.**

BACK TO BUSINESS

PRINCIPLE:
CUT TO THE CHASE

0   123   456   789   0

Power Buyers always try to ask a question, make a suggestion, track a matter or solve a problem in the shortest time possible at the least cost.This may mean that they work the phones before they write a letter; fax a follow-up communication before they send something by courier; ask to deal with a supervisor before explaining their problem to another front line employee.

Trying to cut to the heart of a process has been one of our themes for a long time. The logic of this approach first occurred to us some years ago when we learned how elements of large organizations tend to protect their turf. In the 1960s the State Department developed a new management system to give U.S. Ambassadors better control over the different agencies working out of their embassies. One day a Washington-based Foreign Service Officer arrived at the Cologne airport to arrange a meeting between his boss and the American Ambassador to discuss the system. The Washington-based officer was met by the Ambassador's Special Assistant, clearly worried that the new system might deprive him of his advantageous position. The Special Assistant probed for details. Once he learned that the new system would *add* to his power within the official Embassy community and give the Ambassador another secretarial slot besides, he became very supportive. He could see no impediment to an agreement to implement the new system. At this point, the Washington-based officer said: "We ought to ask the Ambassador to sign the authorization letter now. Look at how much money we'll save the taxpayers if your boss doesn't have to prove how clever he is in 'negotiating' the conditions under which he will accept the new system, and my boss won't have to come here to prove how bright he is at winning some 'concession' or other from the Ambassador." The Special Assistant agreed it made eminent sense. But they also knew that despite the efficacy of the suggestion, both bosses would do the bureaucratic dance to justify their roles.

Faster is always cheaper and sometimes just as effective for businesses as well government. Most companies are bigger than their buyers, and some of the employees of these companies have grown arrogant with the power the companies wield in the marketplace. They can and often do try to outlast their customers. Power Buyers never forget that these employees will get paid whether the customer is right or wrong and whether the employee is pleasant or rude. They know that the status of an employee within a company may depend on how much money he or she can *save* it. Customers, on the other hand, only get compensated for their time and effort through the satisfaction they derive from the result they achieve. Better, then, to get in and out of a transaction to have the energy to deal with something else than to unnecessarily prolong any single quest.

"I would make it worth your while
to dump him now."

CUT TO THE CHASE
Rule: Is This the Right Pew?

Answering questions or solving problems in the shortest time with the least possible cost begins by making sure that you are in the right location and dealing with the right person at the outset of your effort.

To make sure you are talking to the right people, start by pretending that you are a copy editor of the local newspaper. Your first task is to write a *headline* for your story. By reducing all of the sad tales and sorry details of your concern to their essence—so you can explain your need cleanly, clearly, and quickly—you can easily find out whether you are in the right place.

At the outset, then, write a headline for the need, question, suggestion, or complaint you want to discuss with a supplier.Then rehearse the following lines to yourself before you make your first contact:

- *"Hello, I have a problem with* [READ YOUR HEADLINE.] *Do you handle this? No? Do you know who does? Can you transfer me to her (him)?"* Or:

- *"Thank you. I need to know whether* [READ YOUR HEADLINE.] *Can you find the answer? No? Do you know who can? Can you transfer me to her (him)?"* Or:

- *"Ms. Provost, I noticed* [READ YOUR HEADLINE.] *Who is the best person to act on my suggestion? Can you transfer me to her (him)?"*

If you prefer to write a letter or memo instead of making a call, follow the same general rule: Put the HEADLINE in the first paragraph of your letter or as the subject of your memo so that each reader in an organization knows immediately if he or she can help or where else to direct it for action.

POINT: **It is usually faster and less frustrating to try to find the right person at the outset of a quest than to be shuffled from pillar to post as both sides grope to find the right place to deal with the matter at hand.**

CUT TO THE CHASE
Rule: You Can Win a Pulitzer

Once the headline you created has led you to the right person, try to explain your need, ask your question, make your suggestion, or state your problem as clearly and as succinctly as possible. You can do that by continuing your burgeoning journalistic career. Reduce the matter under discussion to statements that respond to five traditional questions:

Who?
What?
Where?
When?
Why?

When you next look at how a newspaper article is constructed or listen to a television reporter deliver a story, note that most breaking events—an accident, a fire, a crime, a proposal—provide answers to all 5 "W's" in the first paragraph or opening phrases of the story. Try doing it yourself. Look out the window right now. What do you see—a car parked, a pedestrian crossing the road, a tree's branches rustling in the breeze? Take a moment to describe the scene to yourself as if you were live on the radio:

"The grey haired driver [who] *of a lovely old deep green Mustang convertible has just parked his car on Glenbarr Road* [where]. *He does not realize a $50 ticket* [what] *will await him when he returns to his car because it is street cleaning day* [why]."

Journalists also religiously follow another rule—the most important information the reader needs is at the start of the story; everything else follows the "lead," with the least important details near the end of the story.

POINT: **Ordinary consumers will be on the road to becoming Power Buyers when they can explain their needs concisely, clearly, and completely to decision makers. It is an essential element of establishing credibility.**

CUT TO THE CHASE
Rule: A Star Is Born

It is not for nothing that actors rehearse their lines and wedding parties walk through their paces long before the public sees the actual play or guests are witness to the formal ceremony. Rehearsal gets it right and makes it look effortless.

It is no different for buyers. If they take the time to *rehearse* what they are going to say—based on a who, what, where, when, and why description of the need, question, suggestion, or problem—they are likely to say it clearly, accurately, and with the appropriate confidence that helps achieve their goals.

Try it. Rehearse quietly to yourself in the car or tell it out loud to the mirror before you make your first contact:

- *"Hello, I have a problem with* [Who—What—Where—When—Why.] *Do you handle this? Who does? Can you transfer me to her (him)?"* Or

- *"Thank you. I need to know whether* [Who—What—Where—When—Why.] *Can you find the answer? Who can? Can you transfer me to her (him)?"* Or

- *"Ms. Provost, my experience with your company leads me to suggest* [Who—What—Where—When—Why.] *Please tell me the best way to get this suggestion to the people who can deal with it?"*

Rehearsal does one more thing. It allows you to refine the *order* in which you want to make your points.

POINT: **Rehearsal doesn't mean it has to come out the *same* each time. A little rehearsal is intended to ensure that you make your points, not that they are letter perfect.**

CUT TO THE CHASE
Rule: Your Time Is Up

Don't give any company or institution you are dealing with more than nine *business* days to get back to you before *you* follow up on your initial phone call, fax, or letter. We got to nine because we counted that many favorite reasons why people **don't** respond to messages, faxes, or letters:

1. The message was never received.
2. The message was lost.
3. The message was misdirected.
4. The message was misunderstood.
5. The message was buried under a pile of other priorities.
6. The message was buried by other responsibilities.
7. The message was forgotten.
8. The message involved unpleasant news;it was repressed.
9. The individual was away from his or her desk—at a meeting, because of illness, on travel.

When you think about these excuses, they are all reasonable; they could be used by any one of us at any time. So if your message doesn't get answered, don't get angry and don't see plots. Assume it was simply overlooked. Start again.

Don't worry about nagging or being a pest. Be one. But do it politely. Remember the old saying about the squeaky wheel getting the grease. Can you remember a time—or recall a field of endeavor—when the one making the most commotion didn't get the most attention? Can you imagine a Power Buyer waiting endlessly for the other side to deign to respond? Moreover, when you are forcing the action, yuou have control of the timing.

POINT: **You deserve a speedy response to your questions, suggestions, or problems. Demand it!**

CUT TO THE CHASE
Rule: A Memory Is a Terrible Thing to Trust

Power Buyers always set deadlines for each step in their quest and then don't leave it to their memories to count the nine business days between these steps; they put them on their calendars and act on them appropriately.

Write down each point of contact—what was said, what the next step or point of contact will be, and when it is anticipated. Here is the little log we keep running on all our encounters:

Date	Contact	Action Taken	Expectation	Next Step

Every contact is noted, every promise recorded, every future date planned. Thus, if you faxed a company on Thursday, the 8th of October, note in your log that your inquiry needs to be repeated on the 22nd—nine working days later— if you have heard nothing in the interim. Remember to put the log in the file you started on this issue. These notes help you build your case and increase your credibility.

***POINT:* Keeping notes is not just for doctors, lawyers, and secretaries; it's for everyone who wants to be a Power Buyer.**

BACK TO BUSINESS

PRINCIPLE:
TAKE THE MONEY AND RUN

0   123   456   789   0

As a general rule, you probably won't be able to get more compensation or a better result the *longer* your complaint hangs around unresolved. Many think that even when a complaint turns into legal action, the same principle holds—that even though more money may be awarded, it may not compensate you for the professional help you needed or the added time you spent to win the award. By tradition, complaints are usually satisfied in terms of the *cost* of the specific injury done, not in terms of the potential loss, mental anguish, or other injustice claimed. Because of this,decide what is due you—so long as you can *justify* the amount as both fair and accurate—and take it when the other side meets or comes close to your expectations.

Power Buyers know that money in hand, not money on the come, is the only kind of money with impact. It is why in lawsuits many people accept the compromise of a settlement instead of the win-lose finality of a trial. They prefer having *some* money to show for their effort rather than take the the risk of ending up with no money.

But no one spends money without expecting something of value in return. While many business people can be just as interested as the consumer in resolving a complaint equitably, business people have a natural aversion to being asked to pay more than they feel is fair or can be justified to *their* superiors—no matter what the consumer's feelings in the matter might be. Power Buyers and business people, like preachers in a pulpit, may not be able to *define* fairness, but they know it when they see it. When Power Buyers are fair in their approach, they know that they are likely to be treated fairly in return and get the money they deserve from any transaction.

*"We'll be happy to give each of you
$100 for the inconvenience—
and a promise that you won't sue us. "*

TAKE THE MONEY AND RUN
Rule: Ask for Current Market Value

Consumers need to look at products in terms of the *satisfaction* they deliver, not in terms of their present economic value. Think of anything you own now—a clock radio on the night stand, the toaster in the kitchen, the lawn mower in the garage. They work for you, they give you service, you know all of their foibles and crotchety ways. They may be a few years old and a little scratched or dented—and they may lack the latest bells and whistles of the new stuff in the showrooms—but you have learned to wonder whether all of the new features are really necessary for what *you* need from this equipment.

To a business person trained in traditional economic terms, on the other hand, used means worn, depreciated, and of less value. That person probably will want to give you the *current market value* of any item requiring replacement. In other words, something that cost $75 five years ago may have a market value today of $40, while its functionally similar replacement may have an $80 price tag. Power Buyers resist taking the $40—they want satisfaction for their problem, not any new ones. Out-of-pocket costs are just such a problem. Power Buyers want to be able to buy the *replacement* without any added cost.

We once ordered a nice gift from a mail order firm to give to our business clients. When the 50 items arrived, we discovered an advertising card stuffed into the package offering a 10 percent discount if the same item were ordered by the recipient. The card had apparently been meant for insertion with *other* products shipped by the same mail order firm. We immediately called and asked that we be accorded the 10 percent discount or we would return the entire shipment for the full *100 percent* guaranteed refund. Needless to say, the mail order firm acceded to our request.

POINT: **Power Buyers measure value in both satisfaction and dollars. If they can't have all the satisfaction they once enjoyed, they certainly don't want to take a monetary loss as well. They usually don't.**

TAKE THE MONEY AND RUN
Rule: It's Budget Time

Most small businesses have to maintain rigorous payment schedules to meet their regular obligations, and most large businesses have budgets that are written and approved once a year. While payment schedules and budgets may be refined and readjusted at various points during a fiscal year, it is sometimes hard to insert additional sums ahead of other demands or into previously fixed categories.

Your request for money in compensation for some problem may come at a time when a small business, or a departmental budget in a particular company, is pinched for cash or even overdrawn. Since you can't squeeze apple juice from the seeds, it is far better to get smart than angry. Ask about the company's payment or budgetary procedures. If you are at the wrong end of a cycle, ask to be put in first position in the *next* cycle; if you are in rhythm with the business cycle, request to have your need included at a high enough priority to ensure payment.

How you ask can make all the difference in the world. We always like to phrase our statements toward this end as questions—they tend to evoke sympathy and bring the other side to your side:

> *"Don't you think it's better and cheaper to fix the timing of a payment now than to leave it to chance or the courts later on? Can we have your commitment that the sum owed us will be paid within the first five days of the start of next quarter?"*

Of course, if this positive and cooperative attitude fails to get you what you want, you always have recourse to other weapons. In the case of crowded payment schedules or tight budgets, for example, the start of a lawsuit is a common way to get your issue moved higher and paid sooner.

POINT: **To get *complete* satisfaction requires you to be as smart as the other side. Becoming smart means being alert to the other person's problems as well as your own. As Power Buyers well know, including the other side's concerns into your approach sometimes proves to be the best way to get what you expect.**

BACK TO BUSINESS

PRINCIPLE:
DON'T START WHAT YOU CAN'T FINISH

0   123   456   789   0

Time cures most things—inquiries and complaints no less than pain and sorrow. Decide at the outset whether the probable energy you will need to invest in any activity is worth it. Big business and large organizations have the resources to remain involved for as long as it takes—a decade in the case of IBM when it was charged with monopolistic practices by the Justice Department.

Big business and large organizations know that they can outlast the ordinary consumer. They also know that many consumers on a crusade weaken perceptibly when the excitement of beginning fades and the first signs of resistance surface to usher in long periods of drudgery. We started a $157 claim for a refund against Laker Airways in *1981*. We diligently stayed with it through the end of the firm's bankruptcy proceedings and finally received the money in 1992.

Only the serious persist to the end. Power Buyers, almost by definition, are always serious when they make a demand. What they start they feel *compelled* to finish. Sometimes a large business—but almost always a government organization—will accept *persistence* itself as strong proof of the validity of the buyer's position. They assume that if someone resolutely stays the course on a matter over a period of time, they need not look very far for other evidence of the justness of the cause.

It happened to us. We were asked by a client to help his sister obtain a passport. Although born in Russia, she had actually become a U.S. citizen when her father received his citizenship. While she had some details about when and where her father had been awarded his citizenship, she had no papers to prove it and no papers of her own. We provided the State Department with collateral evidence from the Labor Department that her father had been through the citizenship process; we produced copies of her brother's naturalization certificate and U.S. passport proving that *his* citizenship was derived from their father; we had sworn affidavits, letters of support, census tract data, and more. We thought we had made a pretty convincing case. The State Department, however, sniffed at all of this. The Passport Office wanted a certified copy of the record of the 1923 court hearing in which the father was sworn in as a U.S. citizen. Luckily, we found a helpful clerk in Brooklyn to do the actual research and authenticate the copy. On our third visit to the Passport Office—and fully one year after we had begun the process—the passport was issued. Because the court records only confirmed what the other paperwork had indicated, we had the feeling that our persistence in responding patiently to the demands of the State Department was itself taken as proof of the honesty of our position.

Because some matters can take a long time to resolve and can whittle away a bank account, Power Buyers pick their battlefields carefully to make sure that the risks they will undertake are worth the reward they anticipate.

DON'T START WHAT YOU CAN'T FINISH
Rule: Make a Plan

Because involvement with a large organization can be complicated, it is always best to make a quick estimate of the amount of time and effort and the likely costs to be incurred in resolving the matter at hand. We usually create a chart to help us organize the details:

By This Date...	Accomplish This Task...	At This Cost...

We suggest jotting down the opening few steps of your plan in the column labeled "Accomplish This Task..."

- Discuss goal with spouse;
- Lay out the evidence;
- Call the manager;
- Get an estimate, etc.

Leave the rest of this column blank to be filled in as the process unfolds and reaction from the other side filters back. Remember, also, that cost encompasses both dollars *and* time. Each must be calculated to make sure that the potential return is worth the investment involved.

Like a chess match, each reaction should trigger ideas for your next several moves. As events unfold, continue to refine your plan and maintain your contact log. (See: *A Memory is a Terrible Thing to Trust*, page 57.) Nothing makes a more impressive case at each step of the process than a detailed recital of past encounters and their results.

POINT: **A plan gets you organized and helps you decide if the result is worth the effort.**

DON'T START WHAT YOU CAN'T FINISH
Rule: Be a Pest

Don't start what you can't finish is another way of saying that you must be persistent. Persistence is not just the ability to remain *involved* over a long period of time; it is also the willingness to become a pest. Bombard the other side with random contacts by one or more people who will maintain a similar line of attack from different angles.

Once when we had the feeling a supplier was purposefully avoiding us, we called his beeper every five minutes and we left messages with his automatic answering service every 15 minutes. The cost and annoyance finally got the better of him. He was forced to call us to deal with our complaint.

Another example of persistence comes when you raise your voice. Too often, though, this wonderfully effective weapon is wasted when someone starts yelling from the outset of a person-to-person confrontation. The person doing the bellowing looks unbalanced, and the listener looks reasonable by contrast. But when someone slowly begins to raise his or her voice as the discussion proceeds, it signals to the other side that the person is very serious and very determined about the issue at hand. Most people, in person-to-person confrontations, become uncomfortable when the person they are speaking with starts to become loud. It allows other people to hear the conversation, and generally draws attention to an unpleasant situation.

If you engineer such a confrontation, indicate to the other side as your voice begins to rise or your body movements become more animated that relief from this verbal pressure and threatening posture is as close as a resolution of the issue at hand.

> *"You know, I wouldn't have to yell like this or get so physically worked up if you would only agree to be reasonable on this matter."*

POINT: **Don't wait to have a free moment to make a call or remind someone of a promise unfulfilled. Call them now. Nag a little. Remind them, loudly when necessary, that your patience is not endless.**

BACK TO BUSINESS

PRINCIPLE:
THERE'S POWER IN NUMBERS

0   123   456   789   0

The more people on your side of an issue—be it a purchase, a problem, or a discussion—the better off you will be in resolving matters with both small and large institutions. We suggest that you start building support for your actions at the very outset. Tell your family, friends, and colleagues what you think you are going to do to resolve an issue. Not only can they offer ideas directly to improve your case, but you can tell from their facial expressions and body language what strategy and tactics may be most effective. Later on—especially if the issue becomes protracted—your position will be enhanced when you can point to a group of people standing with you.

When a client of ours wanted help in trying to rebalance U.S. coffee policy—then starting to tilt heavily to the advantage of the major U.S. coffee producers and away from both consumers and exporting countries—we created the Coffee Consumers Caucus. It was organized out of our imagination; it had no standing other than what we accorded it; it had no formal members, no staff, no charter, no separate office, no independent telephone lines. But it did have a good name, impressive stationery, a background brochure, and us acting as Executive

Director. We told everyone the truth about the nature of the Caucus itself—that participation in its discussions was open to anyone interested in who was being helped and who was being hurt by the Bush Administration's coffee policy. The wonderful thing was that no one really believed us.

People wanted to see a list of the members, they wanted to know who provided the money to pay the bills, and they wanted to dictate the group's future positions. We had created a powerful force out of whole cloth. It taught us an important lesson: People worry about the *potential* of groups as much as they worry about the *potency* of these groups. Even if you only start with your expanded family and increase your group to friends and colleagues, it can still represent a force to be reckoned with.

Businesses, particularly, tend to be sensitive to numbers because volume can do more than any other single element to determine profit. Power Buyers can benefit from planting the idea of large numbers. Try some of these phrases to accomplish the perception of size:

- *By the way, I'm on my way to our tennis club (civic group, business association, alumni meeting) where I think the members would be happy to learn about your firm.*

- *The company asked me to look into this item and to find out whether you (can meet our supply needs, have any other related items for future purchase.)*

When you seem to represent the interests of others as well as yourself, you are automatically empowered with a higher status.

THERE'S POWER IN NUMBERS
Rule: Don't Cry Wolf

We all remember the story from childhood of the young shepherd who cried "Wolf!" once too often to get attention from the people of his village. When help was really needed, no one bothered to come. Power Buyers only start building support among outside individuals and groups when the issue is large enough, the rewards are worthy enough, and the problem is significant enough. The confluence of these three circumstances may be rare.

But that doesn't mean that they stop asserting support for their position. Most know the names of the existing groups and associations that they can alert to their problem. One simple technique, which has proved effective for us innumerable times, is noting who will receive copies of our communications. Nothing seems to generate as much apprehension among business leaders as sharing your view of their companies with the:

- Attorney General;
- XYZ Trade Association
- Editor of the Local Newspaper
- Better Business Bureau
- Chamber of Commerce

If you don't know the names of local groups that ought to be alerted to your problem, start with the Yellow Pages. Look under "Associations" to learn the names of organizations that may be helpful to you. Larger and more complete directories—covering organizations that may not have a presence in your community but are powerful elsewhere—are available in the local library. While those groups and associations might not do anything specific when you first communicate with them, they can be a useful resource in providing information or building a strategy as your concern escalates.

POINT: **Even if you don't *ask* for the help of other organizations, just invoking their name in a telephone conversation or listing them as a recipient of a letter or other material you have produced can be effective.**

THERE'S POWER IN NUMBERS
Rule: The Patience of Job

Most of us know about the legendary suffering and faith of Job—the trials and difficulties he endured as he went from wealth to poverty and health to sickness while never losing faith in God. It is always good to remember that no matter how sorely we are tested by misfortune and bereavement, someone, somewhere else, is probably being tested even more severely by pain that seems to have no connection to his or her own individual behavior.

If the general proposition—that no matter how bad it is for you, someone else is suffering worse—tends to be true, then know also that other people are involved in their own programs, causes, or charities to right even more wrongs and to resolve even greater unfairness. Join them in their endeavors. You will not only help their cause with your effort, but they will reciprocate when you are in need of support. Your strength will increase accordingly.

In a similar vein, a friend of ours keeps notes on the local businesses and suppliers that provide good service and those that don't. She lets each know that she maintains such a file and that she sometimes shares her thoughts with others in the form of a circular letter. The letter not only enlarges her circle of contacts, but it increases her power buying status among the stores and suppliers that want to be sure to end up on the praiseworthy side of her ledger. With today's computers and software support, any individual or business can generate a circular letter or issue a newsletter with an impressive masthead and professional format, including all the appropriate protection embodied in the © symbol. Remember, though, that these types of communication need not have a circulation of more than one—the supplier you want to influence!

POINT: **You can easily create your own special interest group by offering to share in the work of other groups and by asking for the help of their members, in return, for your cause—in person or through a specialized newsletter.**

THERE'S POWER IN NUMBERS
Rule: A Chain Is Only as Strong...

An Achilles heel is not just a phrase we use in everyday conversation, but a real factor to every Power Buyer. Just as the most powerful of the Greek gods had an anatomical point of vulnerability—his heel—so every business and institution has *some* weakness that offers an opportunity for an adversary.

Institutional vulnerability may not be immediately apparent and its character may change from time to time, but it is there. Even those individuals and organizations who seem *invulnerable* by virtue of their position, size, and reach have weaknesses. For one thing, their size can work against them. Large organizations *are* slow, cumbersome, and cautious. Any change has to take into account the individual interests, programs, and concerns of each element within its structure. Ask IBM. Its recent losses have been traced to the company's inability to keep pace with the changing needs of the marketplace. Your opening will become clearer once you start thinking through how speed, agility, and daring can be used to your advantage.

Once you have located a possible point of vulnerability or penetration, exploit it. One of our favorites is to involve radio talk show hosts in our activities. Our effort to force the U.S. Government to break its unseemly silence on the revolution in Romania in late 1989 got us a lot of air time and a chance to ask listeners to send a Christmas greeting to the people of Romania along with a $1 bill (to buy a gift for the recipient.) We asked listeners to send their cards to Romania in care of the White House. While the White House might have ignored that kind of mail, it couldn't ignore the money inside. By law, it had to do something with it. In returning the money to the sender, the Administration was forced to discuss its policy position. The cards had caused a reexamination that might otherwise have been deferred. Sometimes it is easier and more meaningful to steer a few people—your small number of supporters—through a tiny opening than it is to try to bring a massive crowd together to confront an institution's strength. The latter may make interesting television, but the former may get better results.

POINT: **As David proved, it is not easy to beat Goliath, but it is clearly possible.**

THERE'S POWER IN NUMBERS
Rule: Spread the Wealth

While there is strength in numbers, a large crowd in your eyes may appear to be a small group to a major corporation or non-profit organization. When you can't generate impressive *quantities* of people, seek *quality* people to bring on your side. If you find people to join with you who are important or influential to the company or non-profit organization you are confronting, your position becomes stronger. Take an example from the 1992 Presidential campaign. Bill Clinton released the names of 500 of his business supporters. Although relatively few in number, the group had formed part of George Bush's constituency in 1988. The fact that they had switched to Clinton was meant to show that business people in general felt fresh ideas were needed to improve the economy.

A banker in California has long advocated that the Saturday before Labor Day be declared "Capital Day." He has hardly made a dent on the public policy agenda in 10 years of trying. Had he asked us for help, we might have suggested having the *Friday* before Labor Day declared as "Capital Day"— thus creating a four-day, end-of-summer holiday. That would probably generate a number of endorsements—including organized labor's—and at least get the idea treated as a serious proposal.

A few years ago we visited one of the many major theme parks in Southern California. It was very disappointing. When we commented on the experience in a letter, we pointed out the number of visitors who ask us what to see and do while in the area. It was the kind of line that was sure to attract the attention of the theme park's marketing office. In a flash, we had an explanation from the park, an invitation to return at no charge, and two tickets for guests as well.

If you have a problem with a medical supplier, perhaps your doctor will participate in your quest; if you have something that may have legal implications, seek the name of a lawyer to include as a supporter; if you think that the matter you raise touches a much broader group of people, contact a politician for assistance.

POINT: **Power Buyers learn to look for ways to make their case stronger by finding a few influential allies.**

BACK TO BUSINESS

PRINCIPLE:
IF YOU DON'T TELL 'EM, WHO WILL?

0   123   456   789   0

Every day, many of us see ways to correct wrongs, improve procedures, and make life better all around. But some of us are not very comfortable making unsolicited suggestions.

We think the people who read this book may be in this group. Our principles for upgrading ordinary consumers to Power Buyers—in order to let them get what they deserve—are a little like a tree falling in an empty forest. If no one is there to use our ideas—just as there may be no one in the forest to hear when a tree falls—the ideas will have little impact, and the tree will have made no discernable *sound*.

If you have a problem with how a business, non-profit group, or government agency is dealing with a matter, bring it to the attention of the appropriate officials in that organization or to outsiders who can help. Think of yourself as a teacher—someone willing to show others how to grow and develop. The appropriate officials might not express their appreciation for the trouble you went to— even though they should—but you will take comfort in the thought that it is very satisfying to do something that you know is right and may lead to improvements for others in the future.

We had the experience with the Los Angeles Philharmonic Orchestra. Their first annual New Year's Eve Gala—a concert followed by a supper at the Dorothy Chandler Pavilion—was fraught with problems. Because the orchestra's leadership and the city's newspaper critics would have enjoyed the New Year's Eve concert and supper—in different seats and in a separate dining area from us—we thought they should know how the *general public* experienced it. So we wrote a letter to the orchestra's Executive Director noting that "what might have been a memorable event became merely a nice event; what should have sparked unprovoked favorable comments caused …negative ones." We went on to describe some of the problems we had endured and some of the solutions we thought possible:

- *An explanation and diagram of the post-concert arrange-ments should have been inserted into the program—to allow the [audience] to understand what was planned beforehand and to let them adjust their [later] movements accordingly.*

- *…the food tables were too small and too crowded. There was a lot of aggressive behavior [by people] to pile up [their] plates to avoid a return trip. All of a sudden we felt we know something of what it must be like to be in a bread line in Moscow.*

- *There were virtually no seats anywhere in the lobby areas. Did you really expect our more elderly citizens—the vast majority of your audience—to stand through the entire post-concert event, or did you want to thin the crowd through application of Darwin's theory? People had to stand to eat, stand to drink, stand to talk. Worse, there was no place for the ladies to leave their handbags when dancing, and there was no place to put the dirty dishes and glasses. High school gymnasium dances seem better planned than [this.]*

We closed by noting that "our comments are made in the spirit of improving future galas in support of the orchestra's Pension Fund." Ernest Fleischmann, the Executive Vice President of the Los Angeles Philharmonic Association, graciously replied that all of our points were well taken and carefully noted by his staff and the caterers and that they would, indeed, try to do better in following years. We have no doubt that they have. But without letters like ours—or other devices to encourage people to express themselves—would the executives of the orchestra have known what seemed broken and in need of fixing?

There is one other point. Most large organizations invest enormous sums in research to determine what their customers really think of their products and services. It is valuable, but hard to get, information. It is no surprise, then, that those who take the time to *volunteer* feedback are treated as Power Buyers on future occasions.

IF YOU DON'T TELL 'EM, WHO WILL?
Rule: Good Things Can Come from Good Deeds

Scientologists believe that their good turns will be answered many fold in the future. Whether it actually happens that way or not, most of us hope that our good deeds will be acknowledged—perhaps through some kind of reward or recognition.

A few years ago, one of us was involved in a large wedding at a major hotel. The reception seemed organized and timed for the convenience of the hotel staff rather than for the pleasure and pride of the wedding party. So a letter was written to the hotel's General Manager outlining the problems that seemed to need correction. As it turned out, the General Manager had just assumed his duties; the wedding in question had been booked and planned long before his arrival. But to learn more about the facility's operations and to understand better its staff, he personally investigated each of the points raised. He discovered that many were true and that he would need to make changes to have the hotel functioning as he wanted it. In appreciation for the "consultation" provided, he invited us to spend Valentine's Night in their Presidential Suite. Because the suite had its own butler and maid and palatial amenities—two floors, a sweeping staircase and connecting elevator, five bedrooms and an equal number of bathrooms, a gaming room, dining room, and sitting room—it became one of our most memorable experiences. It is hard not to think fondly of the hotel and that night every Valentine's Day.

Whether we are rewarded tangibly or through the satisfaction of having tried to right a wrong or correct a mistake, we view the observations we share and the suggestions we make as a civic obligation—not too different from how we see serving on juries or voting in elections. When businesses are run properly, they prosper; when businesses prosper, the entire community can benefit from an increase in employment, tax revenues, and volunter activities.

POINT: **Finding ways to help businesses help themselves will serve you well, whether through tangible rewards or personal satisfaction. Moreover, you will be treated as a Power Buyer the next time you seek something from the same supplier.**

IF YOU DON'T TELL 'EM, WHO WILL?
Rule: Just Do It!

Nike, the athletic shoe and apparel manufacturer, has used a common human weakness—*inertia*—as one of its principal advertising themes. The company has discovered that for most people it is easier to *contemplate* some great effort than to engage in it. Inertia prevents many of their potential customers from participating in activities that would demand the use of Nike products. To counteract this, the company has adopted an effective slogan: *Just Do It!*

We don't know whether shaming people into engaging in some form of exercise or participating in some kind of sporting activity has worked. But it has pointed out the enormous amount of sloth that exists in our society. People see something that needs doing but can't be bothered.

Power Buyers, on the other hand, always want to be bothered. They delight in the intellectual stimulation of involvement and the sense of satisfaction that comes from finishing an activity. They also enjoy the plaudits that sometimes result from their successful, humorous, or colorful activities.

Some may think that all of this involvement with suppliers is an enormous hassle. It really isn't. If you expect value for money, you must be prepared to spend as much time *after* an acquisition is made as you put into considering the acquisition in the first place. If it turns out that you feel you didn't get value, you have to be willing to put in the time and effort necessary to obtain it.With that attitude, you will not be disappointed.

POINT: **If you do nothing, nothing will get done. Power Buyers have power and success because they do *something* every time they see a need. It isn't all altruisitic. When they do *something,* they gain experience or learn new facts that will be of benefit to them in the future.**

SUMMARIZING
THE PRINCIPLES OF
POWER BUYING

EXPECT THE BEST—If you don't anticipate being treated with dignity and respect by everyone you deal with, you probably won't be.

HONEY CATCHES MORE THAN VINEGAR—Expressing needs politely generally accomplishes more than getting angry or threatening dire consequences.

ASK FOR WHAT YOU WANT—Decide what you need as a buyer from any transaction that you engage in, and you will likely get it.

FIND OUT—Information is your most important resource in getting what you expect. Never miss an opportunity to collect and record data for possible future use.

GET IT RIGHT—When asking for what you want, know all the facts relevant to the transaction accurately and have the documentation at hand to prove it.

THINK BIG—On occasion, consider buying more than you need or hold out the promise of a larger order to win price benefits, increased attention, or better service.

MONEY TALKS—Pay a little more than is asked as either an advance on the full payment due or for the entire transaction itself—or hold out the hope that you are contemplating a generous reward for quality service and attention; give a gift,

...n it's least expected to those who give you continuously good service.

CUT TO THE CHASE—To avoid wasting time and energy, be sure to put your effort into dealing with the people who can make a decision on whatever matter is in question.

TAKE THE MONEY AND RUN—Most transactions between buyers and suppliers should not involve any negotiations; they consist of a simple demand, based on a set of facts, that require only a straight forward yes or no decision.

DON'T START WHAT YOU CAN'T FINISH—Persistence can often be as powerful a tool as the facts in a matter; constancy over a period of time often makes believers of the skeptical.

THERE'S POWER IN NUMBERS—When dealing with larger institutions, be prepared to involve either a quantity of family, friends, and colleagues or a group of high-profile supporters to bolster your position.

IF YOU DON'T TELL 'EM, WHO WILL?—Take pride and learn valuable lessons from getting involved for the betterment of the marketplace and for the good of society.

Tools And Techniques

As noted before, Power Buyers know that they control three important commodities in a fixed-price transaction—their money, their desire, and their contacts. If any one of these is withdrawn before a transaction is completed, the supplier loses a potential sale and perhaps the customer as well. When any buyer is forced to find alternate sources of supply—for one transaction or for all remaining needs—it is at a cost of time and energy. Because the principals of both sides to any transaction generally know the dimensions of what is to be gained and what is to be lost when seeking a common ground, most buy/sell arrangements conclude amicably. While neither may be entirely *happy* with the result, both are at least *satisfied* with the outcome.

Some transactions, of course, do not end this way. When Power Buyers have a suggestion about a product or service or find a problem with either, they hope the seller will appreciate their point of view and respond as quickly and as positively as possible. It is when sellers can't react as Power Buyers would hope—or when they seem to ignore the suggestions or brush aside the problems— that trouble can arise. Ordinary consumers may grouse and grumble about what happens when the little guys are pitted against the giants, but time, space, and other concerns usually heal the indignity of being ignored, patronized, or spurned.

Power Buyers, on the other hand, do not accept these kinds of reactions; they want what they feel they deserve from every transaction they enter into. They also know that they have additional resources—other than the money, desire, and contacts brought to the original transaction—to apply to any on-going effort to get what they expect. But just as it is foolish to use a large weapon to assault a small target, so Power Buyers know how to choose an appropriate *tool* to achieve their goals. Each tool—

Oral Communications
Written Communications
Personal Confrontations
Public Confrontations—

manifests itself in a number of different *techniques.*

The tools are presented in terms of their relative cost—a call is still cheaper to make than a letter is to send, and both are far less expensive than a personal visit. But we also know that some people tend to use one tool over another because of personal preferences and past experiences. Some, for example, invariably put their suggestions or problems in writing—to ensure clarity, to preserve accuracy of detail, and to maintain a record of what has been said—rather than have to try to explain a detailed matter to more than one person over the telephone when patience can erode and nuances can be lost.

"Shall we vote on which tool to use?"

The Tools and Their Techniques

ORAL COMMUNICATIONS
"How kind of you..."
Never Get Angry
Always Get a Name
Confirm Everything

WRITTEN COMMUNICATIONS
Do a Draft
No Distractions
One Page Only
Make Copies
Send It Again
The Simple Letter

PERSONAL CONFRONTATIONS
The Announced Visit
The Surprise Visit

PUBLIC CONFRONTATIONS
A Letter to the Editor
The Press Release
Lobbying
Paid Advertisements
Demonstrations for Attention
Demonstrations for Effect
Boycotts

BACK TO BUSINESS

TOOL:
ORAL COMMUNICATIONS

0   123   456   789   0

Most of us don't think about it with the same wonder as we do computers and faxes, but the telephone is still the most important business machine available for the conduct of commerce. Even though each instrument is now loaded with all sorts of special features—information screens, speed dialing, conference calls, call waiting, call forwarding, and more—it still provides the same reliable service as the black lumps with the spinning dials of pre-deregulation days. If nothing else, the telephone is certainly the most *ubiquitous* business machine available; no organization can exist today without one, and every buyer has access to one.

The telephone, in fact, is the least expensive highway on which needs, inquiries, suggestions, and complaints can be transported to the people who have to act on them. Because of this, it should be the first tool used in conducting any transaction with a business. Before picking up the phone, however, consider how to apply the *principles* of power buying to the various techniques under consideration:

1. Always assume that you will receive treatment equal to that accorded the supplier's best customer.
2. As a result, be polite in stating your needs.
3. Once connected to the proper person, make sure you ask for what you want.
4. Be sure to use every contact with the supplier to develop information that may prove useful later.
5. Have your facts correct and at hand whenever in touch with the supplier. Be credible!
6. Remember to consider how this supplier might react to doing more business with you and your contacts.
7. By the same token, think about spending a little more than you have been asked if the extra money or a gift can be used to your advantage. Always consider what's in any deal for the people connected to the supplier.
8 Once in touch with the right person, stay on the main point at issue until finished.
9. If his or her best offer is close to your objective, take it rather than spend time trying to get the last penny or concession.
10. Be persistent and record the name and reaction of every person you talk to and every step you take.
11. If greater persistence is required, know who else may support your position.
12. Finally, have a little courage: If you don't raise the issue, who will?

Remember the phone requires you to be articulate, brief, and organized. The listener cannot see your body language, react to your gestures, or interpret your expressions; you, in turn, cannot be sure the listener has grasped the points you have made. The only sense available to both sides is *hearing*. So when the other person speaks, listen very carefully to the tone of voice and the audible sounds—the sighs and gasps and mutters—as well as the words being used.

While written communication may proceed in stages—escalating the volume of words or facts to gain attention as the process forces an issue to rise in the hierarchy—oral communication does not work that way. It is, by nature, a repetitious process. From earliest days, story tellers repeated the legends and history of a people to implant a narrative in as many memories as possible. Think of the ads you now hear on radio. Each bludgeons the listener by repeating key information—names, prices, hours, telephone numbers, directions, and the like. The whole ad repeats until the advertiser feels the message has penetrated the resistance, distractions, and competing information that confounds us all. A Power Buyer's telephone call has to do the same thing, and a repetition of the same facts in the same way can help get the message through.

While a telephone call is the least expensive and perhaps the most expeditious way of making your needs known—ever notice how most suppliers will respond to a telephone call before dealing with in-person customers—it is also the least impactful because it is transitory. Once it is completed, it can be easily forgotten. So think of the telephone as a *starting point,* rather than an ending point, in your quest.

Maybe I should call the florist.

ORAL COMMUNICATIONS
Technique: "How kind of you..."

Once Liza Doolittle had finally learned how to say the words: "The rain in Spain falls mainly on the plain" in *My Fair Lady,* she went on to practice her pronunciation of another phrase: "How kind of you to let me come...." We try to remind ourselves to start every telephone conversation with a stranger with variations on that sweet thought:

"How kind of you to take my call."

The phrase tends to soften other people's natural wariness and improves their attitude greatly by hinting at their importance. It works nearly every time. But when that particular phrase isn't appropriate, we have other deferential openers designed to elicit the help and support of the listener. We start with a bright "Good Morning" or "Good Afternoon" and announce our name slowly. Then we start with one of the following:

"This may sound like a dumb question..."

"I'm a total beginner at this, so I hope you can help me..."

"I am sure you can direct me to the right person..."

"I am hopeful you will know..."

Even after being switched for a third time, don't get exasperated having to repeat the same story or enquiry yet another time; this is the first contact with *this* particular listener. Try to keep your voice and demeanor as sweet as on the first iteration. It isn't always easy, and we sometimes forget, but if you use each contact to hone your approach your call should evoke sympathy.

POINT: **Power Buyers know that they have no real power to make something happen on their behalf, only the ability to convince another person to want to help them. It is a goal that can easily be accomplished on the telephone.**

ORAL COMMUNICATIONS
Technique: Never Get Angry

Sometimes it is very hard to do, but the telephone requires a soft but firm manner whenever you need something, ask for something, suggest something, or complain about something. Despite the annoyance, the time pressures you feel, or the perceived denseness of the listener, you must try to remain cool when dealing through this medium. Subtlety—whether expressed as cynicism or sarcasm—is very difficult to communicate to strangers over the telephone.

On the phone, the customer is a supplicant, hoping that someone in power will deal with his or her problem. If those you speak with don't like your approach, your tone, or your attitude they can hang up on you or, worse, ignore your next call. They can also deny you information you need by never finding the time to provide it. If you don't like the treatment you receive, remember that there are ways to get even at some point in the *future*, but that it is unwise to get angry in the interim.

Anger breeds bad decisions. If you get mad, the other person may make his or her decision on the basis of that impression rather than on the facts at hand. Take the unhappy and disappointed airline passengers who confront the personnel in baggage area lost and found offices. *The Los Angeles Times* (December 13, 1992) reported that if the airline personnel really take a dislike to someone they may "Bombay" a bag. It seems that given the problems at one of India's busiest airports, luggage sent to Bombay, instead of its real destination, is very likely to be lost forever.

We, ourselves, have a tough time remembering never to get angry, especially when we are rushed. The trick we try to use to catch ourselves before exploding into the phone is to use a variation of the following phrase:

> *"I'm terribly sorry. It's my fault. I'm not making myself clear. Let me try again to explain my need."*

We don't necessarily believe this particular bit of hoo-hah, but "knowing" the truth has a certain calming effect. We also know that a little flattery for those handling rushed, anxious, or irate consumers—something, for example, those in baggage claims, at the post office, or in customer service departments seldom hear—has a powerful way of getting the attention you need.

POINT: The phone is fast and convenient and may be the best source of information. Use it as such and not as a weapon.

ORAL COMMUNICATIONS
Technique: Always Get a Name

While many people now answer the phone by announcing their names—"This is Ara"—many tend to mumble, others rush, a few speak with heavy accents, some like to give only a first name, others just a surname, a few always use a fake name, and still others tell you their nickname. Double-barrelled names—Mary Jane, Susanne Elizabeth, Wayne Guy, Billy Bob—can create still more problems. Sometimes a name comes down to a question of whether you are dealing with a man or a woman (Robin, Terry, and Darrell always confound us).

Because names are synonymous with one's identity, it is also the most important place to start to humanize your quest on the telephone. If you can bring the other person to identify with your problem, you become more than just a document number, a case file, or a continuing headache. If you can add a title, a department, or some other organizational element to your knowledge of a person's full and proper name, you can also follow-up more efficiently when necessary.

Remember, if you didn't catch the name (Harish? Pejman? Ludi?) or if you are unsure whether you are speaking to Tim or Jim, Tina or Lena, simply ask the person to *spell* it for you. Even when we are pretty certain we have a name right, we still like to ask: "Is your Steven with a 'v' or a 'ph' "? "Doesn't Gisèle come with an accent"? "Is Alan spelled with one or two 'l's, an 'e' or an 'a' at the end"? Both of us know that rule better than most. While Godfrey is a fine name in England, it is not common in the United States. A lot of people think it has to be pronounced as an English Lord might address his butler. It comes out "Gawd-free." Co-author Gregrey has his name spelled on his birth certificate like nearly everyone pronounces it—without the middle syllable. While most people know how to spell G-r-e-g-o-r-y, they usually get a shock when they find out that the spelling of his name has an Anglo-Saxon, rather than a French, spin. While Greg handles the problem by shortening his name, that is impossible for obvious reasons for Godfrey.

POINT: **Never be embarrassed at having to ask how to spell a name to insure you have it correctly. Knowing and using the name of the person you are dealing with allows you to evoke support for your quest and to strengthen your case in the future.**

ORAL COMMUNICATIONS
Technique: Confirm Everything

Ever notice how direct marketing firms take information over the telephone—they repeat everything they are told. It can sometimes drive you slightly crazy if an operator grinds through what is so familiar to you, but may be difficult for someone else to grasp or pronounce.

Operators repeat everything because they have had long experience handling thousands of calls over imperfect telephone circuits. It has taught them how easy it is to inadvertently reverse a set of numbers in a ZIP code, confuse a street name, or mistake 15 for 50.

Along this line, the President of our publishing firm told us about her experiences with our previous book, *Talk Is Cheap*. A syndicated columnist mentioned the book favorably in commenting on the importance of word of mouth advertising for small businesses. Boom! Phone sales shot up overnight as some of the columnist's 15 million readers reacted to her comments. After hundreds of 12- and 16-digit credit card numbers—all said in different rhythms with different inflections and accents—it was amazing how often a 3821 was written down as 3281 or 3812. While the staff was certain they had gotten the number right on the first try, the bank found the errors when the vouchers were returned unprocessed. Moreover, books mailed out were sent back by the post office. The triple-barreled street names, so favored by real estate developers, proved troublesome to the publisher's people. The Americas Group found out the difference between Willow Brook Run, Willowbrook Road, and Wilderbrook Race the hard way. They had to pay the book's postage three times—when filling the order, when accepting the undeliverable return, and when remailing it to the proper address.

We try to remember to repeat our name and address, without prompting, when on the telephone. If we are leaving a message on an answering system, we always give our name and phone number a *second* time at the end of the message. Both techniques prevent errors and help to ensure that our problem gets handled properly.

POINT: **Whatever you say or hear on the telephone, be sure to repeat it or confirm it to ensure your information is accurate.**

BACK TO BUSINESS

TOOL:
WRITTEN COMMUNICATIONS

0   123   456   789   0

If you write it down, it *exists*. There is a permanent, easily accessible record of what facts were discussed, what ideas were proposed, and what agreements were reached. Written communication can be studied and then restudied to ensure accuracy of interpretation; written communication can also reinforce a memory that may miss a detail. It isn't, of course, foolproof or perfect, but it is a major step in the right direction.

While oral communication seems much faster and less of a burden to both parties—questions can be asked and responses received virtually in seconds—it generally takes longer to accurately explain most complex issues than it does to talk about them. Moreover, the nuances necessary to an understanding of a complex issue can be missed entirely in oral communication, but appreciated in a written document. Most importantly, though, what you thought you said and what the other side thought they heard can be vastly different. Short of a crystal clear tape recording of an actual conversation or an unbiased third party witness, the wrangling over who said what can be endless and fruitless.

In addition, of course, written communications can be shared with more than one person simultaneously, thus increasing the impact of your inquiry or point. The simple fact is that most people are not comfortable writing detailed messages or memos—perhaps they fear looking foolish because of a grammatical or spelling mistake, perhaps they find it difficult to express themselves without all the gestures and feedback available in oral communication.

Written communication becomes the Power Buyer's best record of what was said, what was asked, and what was wanted. How the written communication is communicated—by hand, by electronic transmission, or by mail—is not important. The paper trail created in the notes, memos, and letters becomes one of the strongest pillars of support at any point in filling a Power Buyer's needs.

There are no fixed rules for deciding when to write and when to call, but we have a few guidelines that help us decide:

- Open a subject on the phone; close it in writing.
- The higher the level in an organization you need to reach, the easier it is to get there in writing rather than by phone.
- Call if you are testing themes or searching for the right decision maker; write when you are sure of both.

Maybe we should write a letter first.

WRITTEN COMMUNICATIONS
Technique: Do a Draft

It is amazing how often people dash off something in writing, expecting the other side to understand everything that was said. Power Buyers create a *draft* first—checking what they have written on a screen or on a sheet of paper for errors, for completeness, and for the impact of the words they have chosen to convey their intent. Errors are the bane of written communications. They decrease credibility at the very instant that it is needed most.

Henry Kissinger, when he was National Security Advisor to President Nixon, was known to take the first memos from new staff members destined for the Oval Office and send them back for redrafting *without* even reading them. He merely requested his staff person to make the paper "more understandable." The usually chagrined staffer would then labor for hours over every phrase to make the memo as meaningful and interesting as possible. The resubmission would generally be rejected in the same cavalier manner with the command to rewrite it to eliminate everything "superfluous." Again the staffer went over every word and rewrote what he previously thought was as "perfectly clear" as anything Mr. Nixon had ever said. When Kissinger got the third draft, he would call the new staff member to his office and impale him with a glare before asking a question in his gravely voice: "Is this really the best you can do?" If the staffer answered with a defiant "yes," Kissinger would normally smile, read the paper, and send it on. He simply wanted to make sure that anything that went to the President over his initials had been subjected to as much careful thought and hard work as could be applied to the task..

One way to solve the problem of ambiguities, errors, holes, and other problems in written communications is to have the patience to read your written communications out loud to yourself or another person. You will be amazed at how many things *sound* different when heard and how many changes can be made for the good as a result.

POINT: **Remember Oliver Wendell Holmes' admonition: "There is no good writing, only good *re-writing.*" He was right! He knew that care with the written word contributes to credibility, and credibility is crucial to a Power Buyer's success.**

WRITTEN COMMUNICATIONS
Technique: No Distractions

What was your impression the last time you read a letter containing grammatical errors, spelling mistakes, and untidy corrections—especially from someone you think should do better? You were probably both surprised and appalled. Your inclination was either to put off the chore of working your way through the letter or to be disinclined to be reached by the appeal it contained.

We have a friend who is a doctor. By every criterion of what constitutes a *good* doctor—brilliant mind, fine education, superior training, caring attitude—this is a *very good* doctor. But he can't spell worth a toot, and his grammar sometimes borders on comical. Every time we get a note from him we wonder how he made it *to* medical school, let alone through it, and we pray his file notes and prescription slips will not be misunderstood because of his lax spelling and sloppy syntax.

When you are getting in touch with a supplier by letter, the last thing you want is a distraction—anything that minimizes your importance, lessens your credibility, or screens the message you are trying to convey. If spelling, grammar, neatness, formatting, or other such technical aspects of written communication count among the details that you most dislike dealing with, find someone who values these skills and ask for his or her help. If you don't know where to find such a person, call the local high school. There may be an English teacher on staff who can provide part-time editorial consulting; if that doesn't seem comfortable, look in the Yellow Pages under Editorial Services. You should find dozens of professionals available to help. With a fax machine handy, editing can be as efficient as having the person in your own office.

If you do nothing else and you are using a word processing program on a computer, remember to run the spell-check and grammar review. But since spell checks and grammar reviews still miss a lot of what goes into human communication, be sure to read the document over one last time before you send it on.

POINT: **A professional looking and editorially correct communication generally gets more serious consideration than its sloppy and error-prone cousin.**

WRITTEN COMMUNICATIONS
Technique: One Page Only

Never let your inquiry, suggestion, or complaint go beyond a single page. Some lawyers seem to find it a matter of professional pride to be able to puff out even the simplest thought, request, or statement into at least two pages. The American Bar Association reports that the average lawyer in America uses one ton (1,000 kilograms) of paper or the equivalent of 17 trees each year. The rest of us need to make do with only the allotted 75 square inches available on standard U.S. letter-size paper (or the 246 square centimeters on a sheet of A-4 paper). If you don't, you are in danger of being ignored.

We have noticed that when people write long letters or memos, recipients have a tendency to put them aside to get to "as part of their night-table reading" or "when there are fewer distractions." Unfortunately, people often find neither the energy at night nor the requisite periods of quiet to get back to these tedious documents. Moreover, if you want *everyone* in an organization to read what you have to say, you must keep it to one page.

Many will notice that we have created a dilemma for our readers. We have stressed including as many details as possible as one of the principles that will help you win your quest. But details take space and have a tendency to push communications beyond the one-page limit. Because we want it both ways, we have devised a solution. We recommend that you put your key points on the first page

- in
- the
- form
- of
- individual
- bulleted
- statements

and record the *detail* that proves, explains, or justifies each bullet in an appendix or attachment that the reader can review as need arises.

POINT: Sometimes it is harder to write short than long—to say everything necessary in a limited space. We know this well because the format of this book requires each rule and technique to be expressed on one page.

WRITTEN COMMUNICATIONS
Technique: Make Copies

If you think that the question or problem that concerns you may have to be resolved by two or three different elements of a company or organization, make copies of your document and send a copy to each of the people involved. Every time you rely on someone else to do what you want done, you may lose days waiting for them to do it if they ever do. By sending copies yourself, you help insure that every person involved with the problem receives the documents needed simultaneously.

Showing who received copies of a document also has a way of attracting people's attention. One of our favorite uses of this technique is when we are in touch with an out-of-state private company. If we have not received satisfaction from our telephone calls or first letter, then we may add a little eye catcher to our follow-on communication:

xc: The Attorney General

[For whatever it's worth, our consulting firm dropped the convention of "cc" (carbon copy) in its correspondence some years ago in favor of "xc" (for Xerox copy) when sending copies by mail and "fc" (for fax copy) when using electronic communications.]

When a copy goes to the Attorney General, the recipient forms his or her own mental picture of the sort of legal problems that may ensue if the matter is not dealt with expeditiously. When the institution that is proving uncooperative is a public agency, we tend to add copies as follows:

xc: The Mayor
xc: The Governor
xc: The Local Newspaper

Sending copies of your letters should not be a bluff. With the price of a first class stamp and another envelope, you have generated an enormous amount of silent pressure on the recipient to respond to your need.

POINT: **When important people and/or entities receive copies of your correspondence, you can be pretty sure the primary recipient will pay attention to it.**

WRITTEN COMMUNICATIONS
Technique: Send It Again

There is a wonderful scene in the film *Citizen Kane* that should remind everyone to have no second thoughts about repeating an unanswered communication. Orson Welles, playing a character who resembles William Randolf Hearst, is depicted dashing by train from newspaper office to newspaper office as he builds a powerful nationwide communication empire. When he returns to his Chicago headquarters—after being away for what must have been six weeks— his assistant hands him an enormous pile of mail. Without looking at a single envelope, Charles Foster Kane takes the stack and dumps it into the nearest waste basket to the dismay of the assistant. As the Orson Welles character explains, if anyone has written him about something *important*, he will surely write again. The rest aren't worth bothering with.

It is a point we have never forgotten. If something of ours goes unanswered, we simply look for an excuse to send the same communication again. The direct mail experts don't even look for an excuse. They know that the same piece sent a second time to the same recipients is likely to get an identical response as the first mailing. We know ourselves that letters we receive sometimes get unintentionlly pushed deeper into the "TO DO" pile because other higher priority items keep arriving.

Rather than embarrass someone for not replying to one of our letters, we merely try to remind him or her of the importance of the matter to us. The phrase used in Victorian times had it right:

The favor of a reply is requested.

Sometimes, however, when we think our letters are being, purposefully ignored, we send a demand for action in envelopes with eye-catching logos, colorful stickers, and/or a totally different return address. The recipient, usually overwhelmed by curiosity, tends to open these envelopes—and can't help but see our demand for action as a result.

POINT: Use reminder communications, in which you are copying your original, to add some new fact, statistics, or information. It will greatly increase the impact of your communication.

WRITTEN COMMUNICATIONS
Technique: The Simple Letter

To write a basic letter of inquiry or complaint, follow this convenient outline:

1. **Call the company**—Ask for the name and title of the chief executive officer. (Either a mail response unit or the CEO's office itself may channel the letter to the appropriate department for a first-level response. But since the letter is addressed to the CEO, he or she may sign the response or feel personally responsible for the quality of the reply.)

2. **Explain the facts**—*What*, *when*, and *where* something happened, as well as *who* was notified, and *why* this letter is now needed. Use a separate paragraph or

   - individual
   - bullets

to express your main points.

3. **Make your pitch**—Tell the recipient exactly what you would like from the institution in light of the facts you have set out.

4. **Ask for a response**—Be specific about a date and/or location for a meeting or the need for a response to a question. If you would like the recipient to call you, leave your telephone number and the best time to reach you in your time zone.

After drafting the letter and reading it out loud to yourself, ask someone else to read it to be sure it is clear and complete in every respect before sending it.. Once mailed, mark your calendar for when a reply might be expected or a repeat communication may be necessary.

POINT: **Your first communication to a company should be addressed to the CEO, explain your concern, and ask for a prompt answer.**

WRITTEN COMMUNICATIONS
Technique: The Escalated Letter

If after a reasonable time you do not receive satisfaction from the first or second letter sent, escalate the pressure. Keep the tone polite and business-like.

1. **Explain this letter**—Point out the dates that the first and second communication were sent and your reaction to their response (if any).

2. **Re-state the problem**—Repeat the facts: What, when, and where something happened; who was notified, and so on.

3. **Make your pitch**—Tell the recipient what you want and why their response might not have been adequate from your point of view.

4. **Ask for a new response**—Suggest an answer as soon as possible, but no later than nine business days from the date the letter is mailed.

5. **List other recipients of the letter**—

    xc: The Attorney General
           The Mayor's Consumer Affairs Office
           The editor of one or more of your local newspapers
           The assignment editors of local TV stations
           The presidents of interested organizations

Be sure to prepare a little note for attachment to the copies being sent. On these notes, ask the Attorney General whether any laws may have been broken and ask the Mayor's Consumer Affairs Office whether it has received any other complaints about this organization. The note to the media should indicate why you think the story is important and interesting enough to bring to the attention of the entire community. The issue has escalated. Be prepared to follow up with the organization itself, as well as the institutions receiving copies.

POINT: **Be prepared to increase the pressure on an organization if you don't receive satisfaction in a reasonable time.**

BACK TO BUSINESS

TOOL:
PERSONAL CONFRONTATIONS

0   123   456   789   0

If telephone calls and letters seem to no avail—or no one seems in a hurry to resolve a matter you have raised—it may be time for a personal visit to the office of the business or institution. Whether this foray is into a branch office or is directed at the organization's headquarters, Power Buyers assume an attitude in their personal confrontations. They are uniformly:

- Determined
- Organized
- Polite

To be determined, organized, and polite—all at the same time— is not easy. But determination conveys to the people an intention to have answers too long delayed; organization suggests that a plan is in place and no excuse that a document has been lost or a key fact is missing will be acceptable; and politeness conveys confidence that the issue can be quickly resolved once the other side understands its dimensions.

Rather than posing any kind of threat to the employees, Power Buyers view their personal visits as a way of getting *focus* on their problem. It is an "action-forcing process," in Richard Neustadt's classic term for wringing a decision out of a bureaucracy. Personal confrontations put a matter squarely on the agenda and bring the issue to a decision-making level.

PERSONAL CONFRONTATIONS
Technique: The Announced Visit

One of our clients had a problem. She had been billed by the local electric company for charges incurred by a tenant. The bill was for an enormous sum representing some 18 months of electrical use. After a little investigation, we discovered that the tenant company had failed to notify the electric company that it would be responsible for the electrical bills when it took possession of the premises. While our client was indeed liable for the electric charges *before* the new tenant signed a lease, she should not have been billed thereafter. During the "thereafter," though, she kept receiving bi-monthly bills overprinted with a notation that "nothing was due pending a meter reading." She filed those bills away thinking it was merely a computer twitch.

Eventually, the power company obtained access to the meter; a bill in the high five-figures was issued. The client felt no responsibility to pay *all* of the bill. So she paid what she felt she owed and wrote a note on the return coupon. She repeated this procedure for four months. The notes had no impact. So she wrote a letter and *stapled* it to the coupon. Still no impact. Eventually, the outstanding bill—without either notes or letters—came to the attention of the collection desk for action. At this stage we were asked to assist. We spoke with the collection official who only wanted to know *when* payment would be made, not any of the circumstances surrounding *why* the bill was so large. We asked to speak with a supervisor. We were told that that would not be necessary. We were clearly in the wrong place to solve the problem of shared responsibility. We felt that the electric company had been negligent for not insisting on reading the tenant's meter during that 18-month period.

We decided we needed to get the power company's attention. We faxed our city council representative a brief review of the problem and asked *him* to request a meeting for us with the appropriate decision makers at the power company. It worked. Someone with power got the attention we needed. As a result, we had a chance to present our case and to find a comfortable compromise between what was billed the client and what the client felt she owed. At the same time, the power company made arrangements with the tenant to have the balance paid over time.

POINT: **When phone calls, notes, and letters are to no avail, seek a person-to-person meeting to resolve the problem.**

PERSONAL CONFRONTATIONS
Technique: The Surprise Visit

Remember the time when a relative suddenly arrived at your front door expecting to stay with you for a few days? Caught totally off balance, all you could think about was the laundry flung across the guest room bed and whether there was still a cake in the freezer. You felt inadequate, even slightly guilty, at being so unprepared to handle a surprise.

The same sense of disorientation is generated whenever you drop in unannounced on some company with a need that requires an immediate response. Our most ambitious use of this technique occurred a few years ago. A packaging firm in New Jersey had asked us to raise money for them. We sold quite a few of their high-yielding corporate bonds to our clients. For eight straight quarters they paid the interest due on schedule and without problem. Then something happened. They missed a payment date, made an excuse, promised to rectify the situation in a matter of days, but didn't. Our subsequent phone calls were unsatisfying—key people were always going to a meeting to solve the cash flow problem and the meetings were always set for "next week." Our clients were getting worried, and we looked ineffectual.

Finally, we decided the uncertainty was affecting our other business. One of the authors flew from Los Angeles to Newark and drove straight to the packaging company's offices where he told the receptionist who he was and why he wanted to speak with the company president. After a lot of "please have a seat" and "may we get you a cup of coffee" while we "locate Mr. Peters on the factory floor," the president turned up. He cooperated fully, we always felt, because he wanted to know what our unannounced visit might lead to next—a meeting with the District Attorney, a rally for the employees in the parking lot, an appointment with the bankruptcy court to file a petition, a visit to his bank manager, an interview with the local newspaper editor, or worse. He also decided on his way to meet us that truth was his best recourse. He told us in detail the problems the company had been having and how he was solving them. It was so convincing that we even offered to pitch in to help. All in all it proved to have been a trip worth taking. Our clients' needs had risen to the top of the packaging company's agenda, and each received a cashier's check for a portion of the sum owed them. The rest was paid shortly thereafter, and the bonds were eventually redeemed for their full value.

POINT: **While a surprise visit takes courage and energy, the drama created by this kind of confrontation usually makes it effective.**

BACK TO BUSINESS

TOOL:
PUBLIC CONFRONTATIONS

0   123   456   789   0

When a problem cannot be solved over the phone, by letter, or after a personal visit, you can always escalate it into a public confrontation. We see public confrontations in five categories:

- Publicity
- Paid Advertising
- Lobbying
- Demonstrations
- Boycotts

Although we have listed them vertically, they are not hierarchical in nature. They work best, in fact, when they operate horizontally—in combination with each other. Lobbying, for example, is most effective when a paid advertisement appears or when questions are asked by the press. In February 1993, one man in Antioch, California, set out to save a 100-year-old eucalyptus tree from destruction by roosting in its limbs. A few friends provided food and water. The police decided to outwait him. But word of his struggle was passed to the media in the larger surrounding cities. Local television stations picked up the story; national television networks ran the tapes. By the 10th day, the city had capitulated and announced the senior citizen housing project would be redesigned to allow the tree to remain on the property. It was a good example of persistence, group support, and the use of public confrontation techniques to achieve a goal.

Public confrontations need not be a last resort to resolve your problem. The *threat* of a public confrontation can be enormously effective in getting any organization—whether large or small—to focus on a need.

But public confrontations are also generally expensive, sometimes hard to organize, and can be counter-productive on occasion. The decision to go public with an issue—and the manner in which the problem should be presented to the general public—is always a difficult one.

PUBLIC CONFRONTATIONS
Technique: A Letter to the Editor

Letters to the editor may not be read by the people you hope will feel the impact of your words—not everybody works through every part of every newspaper every day. Butletters to the editor are nevertheless enormously effective when they are subsequently distributed.

The recipient of a reprint of a letter to the editor never knows who might have read the letter when it actually appeared or what that person may do with the information imparted. But the recipient does know that letters printed by major newspapers and news magazines automatically validate the subject matter as worthy of public concern. The newspaper may not agree with the point of view, may never take sides, and may not investigate the issue further, but its editors are tacitly telling an influential segment of the public that this subject is worth reviewing.

While every editor has different criteria for what he or she will use in his or her letters column, we have been particularly successful with this medium over the past 25 years. Here are the rules we follow whenever submitting a letter to the editor:

- Make only one point in a letter and make it succinctly; never submit more than 3 paragraphs or a total of about 400 words.
- Try to reference your letter to an editorial or news article.
- Always explain your comment or idea by example or generally acceptable evidence; humor never hurts either.
- Always offer a solution to a problem or suggest an approach for doing something better; never just complain or analyze a matter.
- Always sign your letters and include a current address and telephone number.

Remember that a telephone call to a radio talk show can be just as effective as a letter to the editor because the audience involved is usually considerably larger.

POINT: **It's not where your ideas are published, it's how you use the published material thereafter that counts in making an impact.**

PUBLIC CONFRONTATIONS
Technique: The Press Release

Press releases have evolved into an art form with their own stationery, their own formats, and their own rhythms. Every public relations expert has his or her own favorite technique for catching the attention of an editor and involving the talent of copywriters to ensure publicity about a theme.

Because we use our press releases for a slightly different purpose than merely hoping to generate a newspaper story or capture 90 seconds on the evening news, our approach is also different. Our ideas are in the following release:

NEWS:

HARRIS/RAGAN
MANAGEMENT
GROUP

FOR IMMEDIATE RELEASE
Date
Contact: Godfrey Harris
(310) 278-8037

PUT YOUR POINTS INTO
A THREE-LINE HEADING IN CASE
THE READER DOESN'T GO BEYOND

The first paragraph states why the information conveyed in the headline is newsworthy and of interest to a broad segment of a newspaper's readers or a station's listeners or viewers.

The second paragraph amplifies the information in the first paragraph, but usually puts words into our clients mouth. As Gregrey Harris, co-author of the new book *Power Buying*, puts it: "Quotations allow the authors of the press release to give an editorial slant to facts presented and give readers the impression that a reporter for the newspaper interviewed a principal to develop the information."

The last paragraph tells the reader where more information on the subject can be found.

\#

9200 SUNSET BOULEVARD, SUITE 404, LOS ANGELES, CALIFORNIA 90069 U.S.A.

Telephone: (310) 278-8038   Cable: VALORSA   FAX: (310) 271-3649

We like to distribute the press release to other groups, to interested individuals, even to the organizations mentioned in the release, as well as to the media. One time we sent the release as a "draft." It was sufficient evidence of our seriousness about an issue that the company agreed to resolve the matter before we distributed the final version.

POINT: Press releases are an effective and inexpensive way to show your intent to bring the general public into your struggle.

PUBLIC CONFRONTATIONS
Technique: Lobbying

While lobbying is often thought of as an activity designed to influence legislators in their contemplation of new laws, lobbying has proven equally effective as a means of influencing regulators and administrators in the implementation of laws. But lobbying doesn't have to be confined to the public sector. It can also be used to bring pressure on any private-sector supplier of goods and services to get what you want without negotiations. Here are a few examples of private-sector lobbying techniques:

- **Media Consumer Affairs:** Merely providing a newspaper, television, or radio ombudsman or consumer affairs department with a case puts enormous pressure on a business or non-profit organization to settle a matter and avoid adverse publicity.

- **Stenciling**: While it is illegal to deface currency, it is also startlingly eye-catching to see a bold red rubber stamp proclaiming: BUY AMERICAN on a U.S. one-dollar bill. Seeing any message in an unexpected place—on *sidewalks,* for example—has an unusual impact. If the messages are applied with water-based inks, the chance of backlash is greatly reduced.

- **The Lapel Device:** From the little red horizontal ribbon that signifies the wearer has been awarded the Lègion d'Honneur by the French Government to the crossed red ribbons worn by supporters of greater AIDs awareness, any color, pattern, or shape can be linked to a cause or point of view.

- **The Poster**: Today, messages can be printed and stuck to envelopes, letters, brochures, bumpers, street furniture, or fences or can be printed on quarter-cards to plant in front lawns, stuff in the back windows of cars, wrap around telephone poles, or put anywhere else in public view to make an impression.

POINT: **Any one can mount a private-sector lobbying campaign. Just make sure others know about it through pictures, flyers, press releases, and other means to call attention to the issue and the targets.**

PUBLIC CONFRONTATIONS
Technique: Paid Advertisements

The paid advertisement is often used to reinforce a media message distributed by other means. The usual form used is the one time, full-page ad. While not uncommon in the United States, these ads are a fairly new phenomenon in the European community. Recently, both Coca-Cola and McDonald's came under attack in France as "American" firms. (The American government was then locked in a tariff dispute on agricultural products with the French government.) To avoid a nationalistic boycott of their products, both companies took ads in some 70 newspapers to proclaim their "Frenchness." Coca-Cola told the French public that it is now a "100% French product."

Because the impact of full-page ads is still eye-catching, many have learned to place their copy in the West Coast Edition of major newspapers such as *The New York Times* or the *Wall St. Journal* where circulation is considerably lower than in other regions. As a result, the cost of each column inch is much less. To the organizations and individuals placing the ads, it doesn't matter who sees the *original* when it appears. As with letters to the editor, it is how the reprints are distributed that determines the impact of the ad. Smaller players—those who cannot afford the full-page ad in major publications—should consider taking less space with an eye to enlarging it in the reprints with a banner line that proclaims:

AS SEEN ON NOVEMBER 10TH IN MAJOR NEWSPAPERS.

The most important element of these ads is to gather people to a cause or point of view. Each one not only has to tell a story, but also has to give the reader an outlet for the emotion that the story evokes. While many ads include coupons to clip and send to politicians, most ask for money to continue the struggle. While an expensive form of communication, the full-page ad is a splendid way to call attention to your issue.

POINT: **As with published letters to the editor, it is not the ad itself that has the potential for payoff; it is the way the ad is subsequently exploited after it appears that has impact.**

PUBLIC CONFRONTATIONS
Technique: Demonstrations for Attention

A demonstration for attention occurs when anyone decides to take a point of view out-of-doors. These forms of pressure can be mounted by single individuals or highly organized groups. As an example of the former, we used to see a lady holding a sign at the front door of a medical building across the street from our office proclaiming that a plastic surgeon with offices inside had disfigured her sister. We had no doubt that it gave people with appointments with the doctor pause. As an example of an organized group, members of Greenpeace, often noted for their spectacular efforts in major shipping harbors, chose the 50th anniversary of the introduction of nuclear energy to have a few protestors scale the face of the Sears Tower in Chicago. Not only were the climbers shown on television, but the reason for the protest was given ample airing as well. Labor groups picket unsafe as well as unfair practices. Marijuana enthusiasts in Los Angeles often gather at street corners asking motorists to honk if they believe in legalization. Demonstrations may not change laws immediately, but they did have an impact on minds over time.

Some anti-capital-punishment groups urge drivers to turn on their automobile headlights during daytime hours to protest an impending execution. It is effective as an attention getter—primarily because many of the drive-time radio hosts provide free publicity while explaining the phenomenon to their curious listeners.

The acquisition of one share of stock of a public company gives the holder the right to attend and address the company's annual meeting. It is one of the most effective way to bring an issue before the public and the company's leadership. But before using this technique, always contact the corporate secretary for a copy of the by-laws of the firm to ensure that all the requirements for being recognized and gaining the floor have been met. Have a hand-out available to reinforce your position with those other shareholders and media representatives who may seek more information on the points you raise.

POINT: Demonstrations for attention have increased in number and subject as television has become the prime arbiter of what's newsworthy. Public demonstrations often fill the small screen because they usually show ordinary people confronting organizational giants in interesting settings or making use of unusual props—all favorite elements of television news.

PUBLIC CONFRONTATIONS
Technique: Demonstrations for Effect

There is another type of demonstration—quieter and less public, but potentially as effective. It involves an organized effort to get an institution's attention. Like the old mule drivers who used to whack the animals on the head to get their undivided attention before commanding them to do something, so some efforts are designed to get an institution focused before asking for something specific. In the political arena, some of these efforts are known as dirty tricks—letting the air out of someone's tires to foul a schedule; calling a company's main telephone number continuously to hamper operations. Today in the commercial arena, they are often seen as just plain smart business. For example:

- Filling a company's answering mechanisms with the same message until you get the other party's full attention to whatever it is you want to discuss with them.

- If the company issues business reply cards or envelopes and refuses to deal with you, let them know that you will soon begin expressing your unhappiness by dropping blank ones in mail boxes. The post office delivers these cards and envelopes—blank or not. Because there is a substantial charge to the recipient, they can turn costly when no sale is possible. It won't be long before someone wants to talk.

- We like sending get well cards to business people we think are acting in a strange manner. Implying they are "crazy" and in need of medical care always seems to get their attention.

POINT: **Like everything else at this end of the Power Buyer's arsenal, the most effective techniques are the ones that are used imaginatively. Nothing attracts attention quite as much as attractive ideas.**

PUBLIC CONFRONTATIONS
Technique: Boycotts

Perhaps the most effective form of pressure against a business comes when a boycott of the company's products is launched. Lyndon Johnson always liked to say: "When you have someone by the balls, his heart and mind are sure to follow." So, too, in business. Nothing quite gets attention or changes policy as effectively as a product or service boycott that begins to cut into sales. Remember how:

- The table grape boycott in the 1960s forced an end to the use of certain pesticides and gained recognition for a farm labor union.
- Opposition to nuclear power in the 1970s effectively ended new power plant construction in the United States.
- Boycotting tuna in the 1980s saved dolphins when the major packers refused to handle fish caught by the offending nets.
- Staying away from Arizona at the outset of the 1990s—to protest the State's refusal to declare Martin Luther King, Jr.'s birthday as a public holiday—caused voters to approve an initiative that reversed the legislature's position.

The tourism industry is the target of a new protest—this time against Colorado for passing a Constitutional amendment in November 1992 prohibiting the passage or enforcement of local laws favorable to a gay life-style.

Two phenomena seem to be at work to make boycotts much more effective than ever before. Because political correctness on *environmental* matters has replaced political correctness of international issues, each individual can have an impact today where only the Federal government had an impact before. The growth of faxes, computers, and specialty publications has not only made the task of generating support much easier, it has given individuals access to the mass media that only large institutions could afford in the past. Both phenomena can serve to make even neighborhood boycotts effective and newsworthy.

POINT: **Don't be afraid to think in terms of a product boycott. Sometimes highly localized efforts can make a sufficient dent in sales to force consideration of the issue at hand.**

CHECKLIST OF THE
TOOLS OF THE
POWER BUYER

Oral Communication—On the telephone, be polite, be repetitive, take notes, and confirm everything.

Written Communications—Do a draft, stick to one page, make copies for others, and repeat the original letter with a fresh note if no answer is received.

Personal Confrontations—Prepare and commit to memory an agenda for an announced visit and a detailed plan of potential actions for an unannounced visit before you leave home or office.

Public Confrontation—Practice with letters to the editor and press releases before involving yourself in the infinitely more complex world of organizing demonstrations and boycotts.

CONCLUDING THOUGHTS

As people get older, they come to understand some of the great *untruths* of our society:

- All American politicians believe in democracy.
- Professors welcome challenges to their ideas.
- Your printing will be ready as promised.
- Scientific evaluations are consistently objective.
- The check is in the mail.
- The customer is always right.

It is the last untruth that gets to us. We have found that the customer, when he or she is an ordinary consumer, is as often *ignored* by big business and large institutions as he or she is helped by them. In today's world, the average customer is virtually never thought to be right, only tolerated.

Power Buyers, on the other hand, have discovered ways that get what they expect without negotiations. They do it with imagination. They create ways to solve problems that still allow organizations to abide by their sometimes arcane procedures. Here is an example: We once had a cashier's check rejected because it had been issued by another branch of the *same* bank. The manager said we didn't have an account with the branch we were visiting and under the bank's rules, check didn't have to be cashed. We said fine, would the branch mind opening an account for us? Absolutely not, the manager said. So we patiently opened an account, using the cashier's check as our opening deposit. As soon as we had completed this task and the computer had accorded us immediate credit for the check, we took a check from our temporary checkbook, wrote the first one to cash for the exact amount of the deposit we had just made, and presented it at the teller's window. It was honored because we had followed their procedures. We of course closed the new account and never asked how much that particular exercise had cost the bank.

But sometimes no one—not even Power Buyers—can win. Remember California's 1992 budget crisis? The State was unable to pay its bills for 63 days. Vendors were told they would receive 8-percent interest on the money owed to them as soon as the Governor and the Legislature agreed on a new budget. Eventually, no interest was paid because individual *fault* for the delayed payment—a condition required by a long-standing law—could not be determined.

In another favorite example of how things don't always work out for any of us—Power Buyers or ordinary consumers—an English antique dealer told us how he once acquired an 18th century Burmese bowl hidden in a neighboring shop. On the very day the transaction was completed and the bowl went on display, one of the partners from the neighboring shop spotted it as he passed by. He imagined he was looking at the matching bowl to what originally must have been a magnificent pair. Knowing that the pair would be worth much more than a single bowl alone, he bought it without hesitation at the asking price—a price that was considerably more than his partner had just sold it for.

We know that just as soon as this book is published, some of the rules and techniques we have found useful may have to be modified as some people learn how the power buying game is played by others. While the principles remain inviolate, Power Buyers also know that they cannot keep using the same *techniques* year after year and hope to remain successful.

As a result, continually test new ways to ensure that you get what you expect from the suppliers you deal with. This book is intended as a source of ideas and inspiration, not as an operating manual. Unlike the workings of a machine, power buying has to adapt as circumstances dictate. As we uncover new ideas for Power Buyers, we hope to share them in future editions of this book.

CASE STUDY:
COME FLY WITH ME

We personally began developing the principles and rules of Power Buying many years ago. We had an opportunity to use many of the tools and techniques during a ski holiday to the French Alps. The holiday didn't go quite as the guide books suggest. Here is a reprint of the original letter we wrote some 10 years ago detailing our problems, along with some descriptive comments about how we now view our skills as Power Buyers.

January 8, 1982

Note that we addressed the letter to a person by name along with that person's title.

Ms. Rosemary Aurricio
Director, Customer Service
TransWorld Airlines
605 Third Avenue
New York, N.Y. 10158

Dear Ms. Aurricio:

Moving luggage does not seem to me to present the same level of technical problem as keeping a Boeing 747 flying. Yet your airline, British Air, and Swiss Air managed to make such a total hash of our baggage as to nearly ruin a recent trip abroad.

We recited the facts in the case to establish the context and generate sympathy for the claim we were making.

My family and I left our home for Los Angeles International Airport at 4:00 PM on Thursday, December 17, 1981, for TWA's Flight 760 to London, with a connection to BA's Flight 626 for Geneva, and a ski holiday at Courchevel, France. We arrived at our final destination at 4:00 AM on Saturday, December 19. Total travel time: 27 hours. On our return, January 4, we left our accommodations in London at 9:30 AM to catch TWA's 703 to New York and 303 to Los Angeles. We arrived home at 11:30 PM. Total travel time: 22 hours.

On both ends of our journey, the frustrating, bone-tiring delay in our movement was not caused by weather conditions, mechanical failures, air traffic problems, or other circumstances out of the normal managerial control of TWA, BA , or Swiss Air. Rather, the major problems were caused by inept baggage handling, complicated by personnel incapable of either telling the truth or discovering the facts.

It took us a while to get there, but we eventually let the reader know what the letter concerned.

Here is how a $7500 holiday was almost destroyed by the air carriers:

1. We arrived in London three hours behind our regular schedule, but our connecting BA flight to Geneva was also delayed by an additional three

*Even though three different airlines had a role to play in the saga of our lost luggage, we wanted to establish **TWA's primary responsibility** —since the letter was addressed to them and they were being asked to settle the matter financially.*

While we weren't getting very far toward our goal with each phone call, we were learning facts and names that were helpful in establishing the credibility of any future claim.

The arrogance of big business when dealing with small individuals was hardly ever more apparent than on this occasion.

hours. On the airplane the purser confidently told me how ground staff back in Los Angeles would be running the computers to uncover the connections that might be lost by our tardy arrival. "Don't worry, they'll have you protected by the time you reach London." Having heard that fairy tale so many times before from PanAm, I was skeptical. Well I should have been. No one in London had done a thing about us. Worse, it was a fellow passenger, not the BA personnel, who learned that our original flight was still on the ground and probably makeable. Was TWA there to help us and several other passengers make the transfer? Not a chance.

2. While we easily managed to connect to our original BA 626, we were later to learn that our luggage was left at Heathrow. No one has ever told us why.

3. In Geneva, after all the luggage had been sorted, we were advised by Swiss Air to wait for the final flight from London. "BA will certainly get it out." Standing around the Customs Hall in Geneva Airport after some 22 hours on the road with three hungry and tired kids is not my idea of pleasure. But we resolutely waited until the last flight was in, filed our claims, and left for Courchevel.

4. On Saturday, December 19, we missed our first day of skiing for lack of proper clothes and equipment. Because of the snow and cold, I had to buy some things just to keep us going. Then after four frantic calls to the airport in Geneva, I learned that:

   a. Our luggage had indeed arrived, but our skis were still missing. I asked that our clothes be sent in any case.

   b. Then I was told that our luggage could not be sent by the regular Courchevel coach. "We don't have a contract with the line." BA said they would authorize a taxi, but not a second one for the skis. Send the clothes. "Oh we will, Monsieur, and you can rent the skis." Fine.

   c. To be sure everything was in order, I called BA. Could they ensure that the taxi would be sent? No, said a surly voice, we pay Swiss Air a lot of money to handle these things for us and we

don't interfere. So much for
customer relations.

d. Back to Swiss Air. What time, I
asked, might the taxi arrive? Would
we in fact have a change of clothes
for dinner? Well, said Andrea of
Swiss Air, they were actually
waiting for a Lufthansa flight to
arrive which also had luggage for
Courchevel. They couldn't be sure
of the time of arrival. Would it be
there by morning? Certainly.

5. It wasn't. I called the airport. Andrea
wasn't there and M. Carron was busy. It
was Sunday I was told. I said I was
more aware of that fact than they were.
I waited for the call back. It never
came. Finally, I called again. He
announced that since our skis were
missing, he wasn't sending a thing.
That little bit of arrogance did very
little for my blood pressure. We
argued. He said he would send the
luggage when he could. Could he give a
time of arrival? No.

6. At this stage, I took my three sons to
the village and leased skis, boots, and
poles for the two of us who had planned
to use our own equipment (FF128 or
$23.04) and purchased the rest of what
was needed:
    2 Ski suits
    2 Pairs of ski pants
    4 Turtle neck sweaters
    4 Hats
    3 Goggles
    4 Pairs of Gloves
The cost of these items--obtained from
two different Courchevel stores (sizes
were a problem)--amounted to FF5,654 or
$1,015.92.

7. Let me note that I tried to rent the
clothes, but was told that such a
service is available only in Paris. I
also only bought what was absolutely
necessary for safety and comfort. For
example, two of my sons had their
parkas and only needed pants; I did not
need goggles because I could use my sun
glasses. We bought no apres-ski
clothes: I told the kids to wash
underwear and socks each night. The
soap cost FF5.65 or $1.02.

8. The luggage and our skis finally
arrived late Sunday afternoon--long
after the lifts had closed, but in time
for us finally to get a change of
clothes and some enjoyment from the
holiday.

*When we lost our temper,
we learned how little good
it does. It is one of the great
lessons of life. The other
party must have taken great
pleasure in making sure
nothing was done for us at
the time.*

*In trying to establish the
bona fides of our claim, we
point out that we had not
tried to take advantage of
the situation.*

*By asking for the cost of the
soap powder back we tried
to reinforce the essential
honesty and thoroughness
of our claim.*

I wish that that were the end of our story. TWA, however, managed to lose our skis on the return trip as well. We had hand delivered them to the TWA transfer desk at JFK on Monday, January 4, for the 803 to LAX. It was late Thursday afternoon--January 7--before we saw them again.

I have noted the cost of the ski rentals, clothes, and soap above. That totals: $1,039.98. Unfortunately, there were other costs incurred as well:

Note that we provided complete documentation for our claim to add to its validity.

1 suitcase to hold the extra clothes	$14.48
Duty on $535 worth of purchases in excess of our $1,200 allowance; without $1,015 worth of unneeded ski gear, we would have paid nothing.	$53.35
Long distance phone, tip to return rented skis.	$39.89

All of this totals to $1,147.70. Receipts are attached for your review. Any questions you may have will certainly be answered. Please note that as a public policy consultant, I charge an hourly fee. No attempt has been made here to calculate the amount of time I have taken to assemble and correlate the above information.

We asked for exactly what we wanted—in an amount as well as in the timing.

It is requested that a check in the amount of $1,147.70 be sent to me promptly--certainly in time to meet the arrival of the charge bills due the end of the month.

                    Sincerely,

                    Godfrey Harris

xc: Dan Faure
    GoGo Tours
    6022 Hollywood Blvd., Suite 216
    Los Angeles, Ca. 90028
    Dick Brazich
    Airport Management for British Air
    Los Angeles International Airport
    200 Worldway
    Los Angeles, Ca. 90045
    Doris Clements
    Passenger Relations, Swiss Air
    Swiss Centre
    609 5th Avenue
    New York, N.Y. 10020

By sending a copy to our travel agent, we implied the potential for future damage to TWA's business unless we received satisfaction; by sending copies to the other airlines, we tried to facilitate the decision process.

Despite the problems we had incurred, the episode at least ended on a pleasant note. Not more than three weeks after the letter was written—and well within the billing period of the credit card companies—we received a check for the full amount sought, along with a note of sincere apology for all the trouble we had been caused. We have always believed that our out-of-pocket costs were refunded promptly and without any question because we had marshaled our case so thoroughly as to discourage any counter argument from TWA. We also appeared to be fully prepared to carry our request for a refund to higher levels of the company or to an entirely different venue—a small claims court, for example—if need be. As it turned out, it didn't have to be and we have flown on all three airlines many times since our winter ski holiday to the French Alps in 1982.

CASE STUDY:
COMING IN FROM THE COLD

We have heard how it happens to *other* people, but this time it happened to one of us. A Sears refrigerator malfunctioned so often we were convinced we had acquired a lemon. Here is the saga of how one of the co-authors and his wife dealt with the matter:

June 21, 1990

Manager
Sears—Major Appliance Division
Sears Tower
Chicago, IL 60606

Dear Sir:

As you can see from the enclosed [receipts] we have had a lot of service calls on our Sears refrigerator. The thermostat has been replaced 2 or 3 times; the icemaker has been replaced; and the "frozen drain" has now been unclogged 3 times.

The Service people have been courteous, efficient, kind, understanding, professional and experienced, but we still have the same problem. Sears is spending a lot of time and money and--unfortunately--it is taking its toll of my workday and presence of mind.

It is possible that we have in fact a "lemon." My vegetables and fruits freeze; leftovers freeze; milk and butter freeze; water drips and freezes.

Please contact your local maintenance supervisor to either effect a prompt and complete repair--or order a new appliance. Thank you.

Sincerely,

Barbara D. Mayer

PS. Would add that we have a Sears washer, dryer, and separate standing freezer which have all performed beautifully over the years.

Frustration with local Sears officials—who didn't seem to care—sparked the letter to Sears national headquarters in an appeal for action.

Barbara D. Mayer is Godfrey Harris's wife.

A way of suggesting that valuable future business could be lost.

About three weeks later, Mayer received a letter from the Sears National Customer Relations Manager. He said that the letter "...had been forwarded to a Company executive in [her] vicinity, who has the authority and responsibilty to resolve this matter." By the end of August, it wasn't resolved. The following memo was designed to escalate the pressure:

August 31, 1990
via FAX (818) 882-8659
@8:15 AM

> To: Ms. Gerri Gordon
> Manager, Sears Service Center

> From: Godfrey Harris (husband of
> Barbara Mayer)

Subject: **REFRIGERATOR!**

The complaint was stated.

We have been extremely disappointed with the service provided by your department and by Sears. Yet again another repair person has failed to fix the problem with our refrigerator—as of this morning it *still* doesn't work.

The problem was reviewed and a little "put yourself in our place" sympathy was sought.

No one who purports to sell service contracts—as Sears does—can claim to fulfill its contractual obligation when *four* different repairmen in the span of *two* weeks are not only unable to repair a Kenmore refrigerator but are unable even to agree on the source of the continuing problem. No customer should have to go 14 days with the *noise, smell, filth, and/or inconvenience* involved when a house becomes a repair shop. Would you put up with it if you were the suffering party?

So here is what we **require** (and the word "require" is not used lightly after 14 days of being without a working refrigerator):

The need was expressed, as precisely as possible, but we should have used the refrigerator's serial number for complete identification.

EITHER WE ARE GIVEN A PROPERLY FUNCTIONING LOANER REFRIGERATOR (BY TOMORROW) OF EQUAL SIZE AND QUALITY TO THE ONE WE HAVE IN OUR HOUSE WHILE OUR REFRIGERATOR IS TAKEN TO A SHOP TO BE FULLY REPAIRED, COMPLETELY TESTED, AND RETURNED PROPERLY CLEANED AND IN WORKING ORDER...

                    OR

A repairman had dropped the potentially valuable information that Sears bills the original manufacturer for each service call.

WE ARE GOING TO BUY ANOTHER REFRIGERATOR, BRING SUIT AGAINST SEARS FOR ITS VALUE AND OTHER DAMAGES WE HAVE SUFFERED, AND CONTACT BOTH GE AND WESTINGHOUSE TO LET THEM KNOW EXACTLY WHAT THEY HAVE BEEN PAYING FOR.

I expect to hear from you by phone or FAX today.

In responding to our demand, Sears called the next day to ask whether anyone would be at home at 3:00PM to accept delivery of a loaner refrigerator. They said that they wanted to remove the Kenmore for repair in their own shops. But, unfortunately, the saga didn't end there. After three weeks of suffering with an inadequate loaner refrigerator, we had to send another memo.

September 22, 1990
via FAX (818) 882-8659

To: Ms. Gerri Gordon
    Manager, Sears Service Center

From: Godfrey Harris (husband of
      Barbara Mayer)

Subject: **NOW WHAT?**

*The problem is again
stated upfront so the
reader has no doubts
about the issues.*

At first blush, it strikes us as somewhat
ironic that a refrigerator you tried to fix
four separate times over a span of 14 days in
the middle of our kitchen floor has been under
repair in the heart of your workshop for 21
days to no apparent avail. It may well be that
the problems we have experienced with the
machine over the last 8 months are proving
intractable.

*This time humor was
tried...*

Since our last exchange on August 31, 1990,
though, we have not heard one word from any of
your refrigerator doctors or their supervisors
about the problems our refrigerator is suffering, its prognosis, or your interest in putting
it in a convalescent hospital.

*...as well as a little
topicality.*

At second blush, however, it is beyond annoying
now to still be dealing with a loaner refrigerator that sounds like a covey of cooing
pigeons every time its door is opened and that
manufactures ice around its freezer department
at a rate to make it a potential national
treasure. Sears should airlift it to our troops
in Saudi Arabia—it could keep a company of the
82nd Airborne in chipped ice until the Persian
Gulf crisis ends.

May we hear from you about our refrigerator
with a plan for proceeding, or will we have to
take further extraordinary measures to resolve
the problem?

A few days later, the repaired refrigerator was returned, and the loaner was removed. But still the problems did not end. The refrigerator had a broken heater cover when returned. Barbara Mayer sent a memo by fax to the Sears Appliance Manager, the Service Technical Manager, and the Service Center Manager. After reviewing all the past history she made these points:

*The log maintained on this
matter made the chronology
easier to reproduce when
needed.*

On October 1, 1990, our refrigerator was
returned with a broken heater cover. A repairman made appointments for 10/30 and 11/3 and
did not show for either. In the meantime, the
operation of the refrigerator has returned to
its previous state last August--milk is
freezing and ice cream is defrosting.

Note the point involving consumer affairs was saved to add additional pressure.

> In August my husband said either we get it repaired or we sue Sears for the cost of a new appliance. He also said he would alert GE and Westinghouse concerning the service being charged. Now he wants to escalate his anger to Consumer Affairs officials in Sacramento.
>
> It is beyond time for palliatives. It is time for you to act today or explain your operation to a lot of outsiders in a week or two. If one of you is not in touch with us today with a solution, we will assume your answer.

No response. The next weekend, Mayer and Harris purchased a new GE refrigerator to replace the Kenmore. True to her promise, Mrs. Mayer also entered suit against Sears Roebuck & Co. and Sears Product Services on November 28, 1990, in the Small Claims Division of the Van Nuys Branch of the Los Angeles Municipal Court. She alleged that Sears had breached its maintenance agreement by failing to furnish "...service necessary to maintain the proper operating condition..." of her 1984 refrigerator. She asked for $834.96 in damages. Trial was set for January 16, 1991.

But the trial never took place. Between Christmas and New Years, a Sears official suggested settlement. He asked how the claim of $834.96 had been established. A copy of the calculation notes was sent to him:

> Assuming the average life of a refrigerator to be 14 years, the Kenmore provided only 55 months of worthwhile service. As a result, 67% of the value of the original refrigerator is sought: $546.38
>
> Because one-half of the term of the maintenance agreement on the Kenmore would no longer be needed, a 50% refund of its cost is sought: $72.08
>
> When the refrigerator was removed for repair in Sears own facility, a line connecting the ice maker to a water source was damaged. Sears is asked to refund that charge: $206.00
>
> Line charges to send Sears faxes during the protacted effort to have the refrigerator repaired cost: $10.50

Note the detail. It suggests that the numbers were devised with care and with no effort to puff the total.

Sears officials said that while they might quibble with some of the assumptions, they didn't think it was beneficial to prolong the struggle. On January 3, 1991, we received a check for $834.96, the old Kenmore—kept as potential evidence for the trial—was taken away, and the matter was finally closed.

ALPHABETICAL INDEX OF RULES AND TECHNIQUES

ABOUT THE AUTHORS

After publication of *Talk Is Cheap*—a book devoted to helping businesses develop ways to actively engage *customers* in promoting their products and services—the authors began looking at businesses from the *buyer's* side of the cash register. What incentive would buyers have to promote a product or service through word of mouth? It was not long before they realized that they could divide customers into two groups: Power Buyers and ordinary consumers. They identified Power Buyers as those who would likely be involved in generating positive word of mouth and might be a danger if their comments turned negative. They noticed that when ordinary consumers began actively promoting businesses through word of mouth they started to sound like Power Buyers. But something was missing. They didn't seem to know exactly how to get everything they wanted from the purchases they were making.

So the authors began talking about what it would take to elevate an ordinary consumer to the same level as a Power Buyer. When they defined what they meant by the term "Power Buyer," they realized that they themselves qualified for the designation because they had developed and refined many principles and techniques that always seemed to work in getting what they expected.

In exchanging notes and ideas, the authors—a father and son team—realized that their widely different experiences in life and business could make a book on how to become a Power Buyer of interest. Here is a brief sketch of the background they brought to this task:

Godfrey Harris, the father, has been a public policy consultant based in Los Angeles, California, for the past 24 years. He began consulting after brief careers as a university lecturer, an intelligence officer in the U.S. Army, a Foreign Service Officer with the State Department in Bonn, London, and Washington, DC, and a management analyst in the Office of Management and Budget. As President of Harris/Ragan Management Group, he has focused his consulting activities on tourism development, commemorative events, and product development. He holds degrees from Stanford University and the University of California, Los Angeles.

Gregrey J Harris, the son, specializes in direct marketing. He began his business career operating his own photography business dedicated to providing legal evidence and managing major accounts for Harris/Ragan. Later he conducted market analyses and developed a data base for cable television's FNN network. In 1988, Harris became a direct marketing program manager for Hewlett-Packard. In 1992, he was appointed a Direct Marketing Manager in the Information Systems Division of Hyundai Electronics America. He holds a BA in economics from the University of California, Santa Barbara, and an MBA in both marketing and finance from the University of Southern California.

As always, the two understand that while a book may begin from a single question or a single line of reasoning, it eventually must encompass the talents and ideas of a wide range of people if it is to be successful in the marketplace. We have again been able to bring together a team of supportive and talented people to help us polish and refine this book. They are:

Nancy Boss Art—An editor who tells us what she thinks of our spelling, syntax, grammar, and organizational skills and then corrects everything that is wrong with what we do.

Kennith Harris—A school teacher in real life, but a computer authority at other times, he installed and maintained the hardware and software used in the preparation and publication of the book.

Jamie Pfeifer—A talented cartoonist who has been involved in the design of our covers in the past and who again lent his skill to the one you see on the front of this book.

Sergei A. Diakonov—This Russian architect and designer from the town of Velikiye Luki suggested the use of a credit card design motif to introduce each Principle and Tool as a way of highlighting the fact that the *consumer* holds the ultimate power over a business.

We also again extend our appreciation to the many relatives and friends— **William P. Butler, Sandrine Chaumette, Suzanne Clark, Eve Dutton, David Harris, Mark Harris, Michael Harris, Victoria Harris, Siu Po Lee, Shirley Lister, John Marks, Barbara DeKovner-Mayer, John Powers, Michaelyn Provencio, and Peggy Wand**—who read all or portions of the book, contributed suggestions, provided help, or gave us their own ideas about power buying.

Godfrey Harris
Los Angeles, California
Gregrey J Harris
San Carlos, California

March 1993

INDEX